THE LADIES' LOUNGE

Josef Slonský Investigations Book Eight

Graham Brack

Also in the Josef Slonský Series
Lying and Dying
Slaughter and Forgetting
Death on Duty
Field of Death
A Second Death
Laid In Earth
The Murdered Molls

THE LADIES' LOUNGE

Published by Sapere Books.

224 Trafalgar Road, Ilkley, LS29 8HH,
United Kingdom

saperebooks.com

Copyright © Graham Brack, 2025
Graham Brack has asserted his right to be identified as the author of this work.
All rights reserved.

No part of this publication may be reproduced, stored in any retrieval system, or transmitted, in any form, or by any means, electronic, mechanical, photocopying, recording, or otherwise, without the prior written permission of the publishers.
This book is a work of fiction. Names, characters, businesses, organisations, places and events, other than those clearly in the public domain, are either the product of the author's imagination, or are used fictitiously.
Any resemblances to actual persons, living or dead, events or locales are purely coincidental.

ISBN: 978-0-85495-735-4

CHAPTER 1

Prague, Czech Republic, 2009

The phone call that came in was terse. That kind usually was, Captain Josef Slonský reflected. It led him and Lieutenant Jan Navrátil to a small top floor flat not far from the Old Town Square in the middle of Prague. There was no response to the detectives' knock, so Navrátil suggested forcing the door.

'You can try,' Slonský commented, 'but this isn't a 1970s Communist-era door. This one has been here longer than I have. You'll just bounce off.'

Navrátil, being slight of frame, had been hoping that his boss was going to do the barging of the door, but that would have involved Slonský doing some exercise, and while most medical opinion was that exercise was not known to be injurious to health, Slonský would beg to differ.

'What will we do then?' Navrátil enquired.

'You go to the top of the stairs and keep a lookout,' Slonský instructed, fishing in his pocket for a little toolset a reformed burglar had once given him, along with a complimentary training course in its use. In a few seconds there was a rewarding *clunk* from the door, which swung open. Navrátil silently handed Slonský a pair of gloves, reasoning, correctly, that Slonský would have forgotten to bring any.

'What does your nose tell you?' Slonský asked.

Navrátil inhaled deeply. 'Not good,' he said. 'Something smells very dead.'

'I'm glad you've said that. I was just thinking that it was time to get this suit cleaned.'

Navrátil eased open the door to the first room on the right and carefully stepped inside. It was a bedroom containing a double bed, a wardrobe, a chest of drawers, a valet stand on which a navy jacket and matching trousers were draped, and a door opening onto a closet in which shirts, sweaters and underwear were carefully folded.

Navrátil glanced at the labels. 'All seem to fit the same person,' he remarked.

Slonský opened the door opposite, revealing a spotless kitchen complete with a knife block containing all the expected knives, a rack with a set of matching saucepans and a basket of bread rolls that were beginning to look a little green.

The next door on the right was obviously a toilet, pristine and equipped with a small basin and an expensive hand towel hanging on a ring attached to the wall. Beyond that there was a rather old-fashioned bathroom with a heavy tub resting on elegantly shaped lion's feet and then a small guest bedroom containing a single bed and an item of furniture that Slonský would have described as a wardrobe with drawers beneath. It was empty. Directly opposite the front door was a utility room that housed the boiler and a clothes horse on which laundry was airing. It was long since dry.

There remained two doors on the left. The one alongside the kitchen proved to be a small study. It had probably been designed as a dining room and could return to its original use if the gateleg table in the corner was dragged to the centre and opened out. A large, rather elderly leather chair stood in front of a desk, and there were some freestanding bookshelves.

The final room was furnished tastefully with two sofas at right angles, a small television, and a large woollen rug complete with a dead man lying on his back. His head looked asymmetrical.

'I'd better send for the pathologist,' said Navrátil.

'Good idea,' agreed Slonský. 'That's what I'd do. A chiropodist wouldn't be nearly as useful.'

Navrátil took out his mobile phone and stepped into the corridor.

'It's okay,' Slonský assured him. 'I promise not to interrupt while you're talking to Novák.'

'Force of habit,' Navrátil replied before speaking briefly on the phone. 'Dr Novák will bring a crime scene team too.'

'That's handy. That's exactly what we need,' Slonský mumbled. 'Well, we can't do much until they come. I'll stay here and guard the body while you go and get some coffee and pastries. We may be here some time.'

Dr Novák crouched by the body and took some measurements. 'No obvious weapon here. It looks like the killer came equipped.'

'Not a lot of blood, considering,' Slonský remarked.

'There will be when I open his skull,' Novák replied. 'I'm pretty sure he's got a large intracranial bleed.'

'You reckon?'

'Yes, probably caused by a hefty clout with a broad blunt object. I'll know better when I get him into the mortuary but my initial thought is that someone has hit him on the head with a spade.'

'Not subtle then.'

'About as subtle as a spade to the side of the head.'

Slonský nodded thoughtfully. 'Taller than him? Shorter?'

'Unless I know whether the victim was standing, sitting or lying when struck, I can't answer that one.'

'Any idea on time of death?'

'Slonský, I can't even tell you the date of death, let alone the time. We may need a forensic entomologist.'

'A what?'

'Someone who can identify these maggots. That'll tell us a bit more. But I'll be surprised if it's less than a week. I can do some biochemical decomposition analysis.'

'Is that a posh way of saying you'll work out how long he's been going off?'

'More or less. But more dignified.'

Slonský paced the room impatiently.

'Slonský, this is going to take some time, and I can't do it any quicker if you keep getting in my light. Why don't you go and help Navrátil?'

'He's going door to door in the building. He doesn't need me. There aren't that many flats.'

'Then go through that desk next door and find out who this man is. Or go and have a coffee. Basically, do anything other than what you're doing now.'

'But I'm hanging on your every word.'

Novák gave Slonský a pair of new words to hang on, the second of which was "off".

Navrátil returned to find his chief gazing out of the study window. 'Is there something of interest in here?' he asked.

'I don't think so. I'm just keeping out of Novák's way. He's in a funny mood.'

Knowing Novák as he did, Navrátil found that hard to believe. 'They've traced the phone call to a public call-box near the Metro station.'

'Any information on the voice?' asked Slonský.

'No. The smell can't have been good for a while. Why wait a few days and then call at four o'clock on a Friday afternoon?'

'Media value. We'll get here, probably close the road outside, cause traffic chaos at the busiest time of day and there's just enough time to get it on the evening news. Somebody wants someone to know this has happened.'

'You think the killing was a warning to others?'

'Or an announcement that they've sorted something out. Who knows? Any information about the deceased?'

'It seems his name was Vitek; Dominik Vitek, and —' Navrátil broke off, because Slonský was no longer listening. Upon hearing the name he had marched through to the room where Novák was still crouched over the body.

'Does the name Dominik Vitek mean anything to you?' he demanded.

Novák blinked in confusion. 'Yes, but why are you asking me now?'

'This is his flat, so presumably this is him.'

Novák stepped back to take a better look. 'He's gone downhill a bit if it is.'

'It's been the best part of thirty years, Novák. He's put on a bit of weight and gone bald, but now that the name has been mentioned, I can see it. Look at the area around the eyes and nose.'

Novák made a frame with his hands to block out the rest of the face. 'I see what you mean. It could be, couldn't it? But let's not jump to conclusions.'

Slonský turned to Navrátil. 'Let's see if we can turn up any recent photos of Dominik Vitek in life, lad, just to be on the safe side. Get Krob onto it.'

'He'll have gone home, sir.'

'Of course he'll have gone home. But he can get the Metro back, can't he?'

'I could ask Lieutenant Peiperová?'

Slonský sighed theatrically. 'Navrátil, you're married to Kristýna. You're allowed to use her first name.'

'Unprofessional at work, sir.'

'Have it your way. But she and Jerneková have enough on their plate at the moment, sorting out the public transport scam.'

'What's that then?' Novák wanted to know.

'You don't travel by public transport,' Slonský pointed out. 'You have that big German gas-guzzler and probably a private train for all I know.'

'How do you think I got here? There's nowhere to park in these back streets.'

'Fair point. It's that old scam revived — people pretending to be ticket inspectors and demanding on-the-spot fines from tourists. Except that these really are ticket inspectors and they've got accomplices in the ticket halls watching for tourists who don't know they have to validate their tickets before use. They phone through a description to inspectors on the platform so they know who to challenge.'

'Shifty, but isn't it legal?'

'Not if they pocket the fines. The tourists don't get any receipt. Still, we've got some names now thanks to Jerneková so they're are busy rounding them up.'

'What did Jerneková do?'

'Got on a Metro without visibly stamping her ticket. The goon challenged her, so she flashed her police badge and handcuffed him to one of the poles in the carriage. The two of them spent a long day going back and forth along line C until his memory was jogged a bit. She was okay. She had a seat and a backpack full of snacks and a book to read.'

'Nothing like being prepared.'

'She's a good girl. A good policeman. Policewoman. Policeperson. Whatever.'

Navrátil was frowning.

'And Peiperová is a good girl, too,' Slonský added. 'So are you, Navrátil. Happy now?'

'I was hoping you were going to enlighten me on who this fellow Vitek is.'

'Let's go through to the study and I'll explain. I think you're annoying Novák.' Slonský wrapped an arm round Navrátil's shoulder and steered him to the study where he offered Navrátil the chair and perched himself on the edge of the desk. 'Long, long ago,' he began, 'when you were just a twinkle in your dad's eye, some nasty people called Communists ran this country. During the Seventies a dissident movement started up and eventually there was a thing called Charter 77 drawn up, which was a sort of petition demanding human rights like they had in the West. Rights which, incidentally, the government had signed up to providing and then done nothing about. Because Charter 77 wasn't an organisation as such, the government couldn't easily crack down on it. It didn't have any offices to close or leaders to chuck in prison, which were the two principal tactics normally used by the State Security Service, the StB.'

'And Vitek was one of the signatories?'

'I don't know, but some of the meetings took place where he worked. He ran a little cabaret bar then which specialised in political satire.'

'And he wasn't shut down?'

'Frequently, but he'd just move and start again. I went once or twice. The vodka was cheap there, so I don't actually remember much about the content of the show. Anyway, when the Wall came down Vitek was smart enough to realise that political satire needs a target and now that the opposition was in charge he didn't really have one. Not straight away, anyway. So he sold his main cabaret and started opening little nightclubs. He had a comedy club and a jazz club, neither of them too big but with good regular customers.'

'Wasn't there some strife between the nightclub owners a while back?'

'Yes, but that was where Vitek was clever. He was an old-fashioned man with a hankering for the inter-war years. He decorated his clubs like places in the Twenties and he didn't go in for some of the stuff that the strip-clubs did. I'm not saying that his places were the sort of club you could meet your priest in, but they weren't as tawdry as some. The girls could actually dance, and some of them could sing. He also opened one of Prague's first women's members' clubs.'

'With male dancers?'

'No, just a safe space for women to meet. Needless to say, that only applied to women who could afford the membership fees and the price of the drinks, but you wouldn't get hassled there, and he employed some of the biggest, meanest bouncers in town to make sure that no drunk lads who wanted to try their luck could get in. If I remember correctly, part of the deal was that he laid on a taxi home for his customers, and if any of the drivers got frisky the taxi company lost all his business, and everyone knew that. So it was where the most successful women and the wives of the most successful men wanted to hang out. Never mind that the fizz cost twice as much as anywhere else. Now, what was the place called again?'

Novák called through from the next room.

'The Ladies' Lounge.'

'Have you got ears like satellite dishes?' Slonský shouted back. 'It's just as well we weren't talking about you if you're going to eavesdrop.'

'I wasn't eavesdropping. If you didn't want me to hear you have to keep your voice down.'

Paranoid, Slonský mouthed silently to Navrátil. 'Thinks we've got nothing better to do than talk about him.'

'So is The Ladies' Lounge still going? I can't say I've heard of it.'

'Not that I know of. It had its day, did well in the first ten years or so, but then came the recession at the end of the Nineties and suddenly people didn't have that kind of money to spend. Anyway, Vitek would have been a fair age by then and ready to retire. He wasn't equipped to argue with the hoodlums who were opening clubs in competition, so he probably just sold up and lived off the proceeds and his state pension.'

Navrátil looked about him. 'It doesn't look like he was struggling.'

'It's like my mum used to say, "If you buy quality in the first place it lasts". I don't see anything here he must have bought recently.'

'Sir?'

The voice came from a plastic-suited technician in the doorway.

'Look, Navrátil!' said Slonský. 'A condom with a man inside.'

'Sirs, have either of you touched the pan rack in the kitchen?'

'No,' answered Navrátil.

'Why do you ask?' Slonský wanted to know.

'Well, I might be wrong, but the gentleman who lived here appears to have been obsessively tidy. But if you look at the pan rack, one pan's handle isn't lined up with the others. I wondered if it might be the murder weapon.'

Slonský pushed past to see for himself. It was as the technician had described; three saucepans with the handles pointing to six o'clock, and one pointing to four o'clock.

'Have you checked for prints?'

'Clean as a whistle, sir.'

Slonský picked up the large frying pan and weighed it in his hand. 'That's got to be three kilos or more,' he muttered. 'You could do someone some damage with this.'

'I'll check it over for tissue residue,' said the technician.

'Good spot,' Slonský told him, then turning to Navrátil said, 'Why didn't you see that?'

'You were the one who opened the kitchen, sir.'

'Was I?'

'Yes, sir.'

'I'd have got round to it when we'd finished in the study, no doubt. When we get back to the station let's see if we can find Vitek's next of kin. Aren't you going to make a note of that?'

'I'll remember,' Navrátil assured him.

'Are you sure?'

'Yes, sir.'

Slonský was fixated on memory because he had recently suffered an accusation from his drinking buddy Valentin that his memory was failing, Slonský having forgotten to take his wallet to the bar where they were meeting. His defence had been that he hadn't forgotten his wallet at all; he had forgotten his raincoat, in which his wallet happened to be. But since that encounter he had subjected himself to a prolonged assessment during which he had written down all the times that he had forgotten something during the month. Fortunately, he had then forgotten where he had put the list.

Novák was walking past the door when Slonský hailed him.

'Not finished already?'

'Just putting my bag back in my car. I'll come and talk to you about it all once I've done that and supervised the removal of the body.'

Slonský sighed. It was going to be a long evening. 'That place where you got the pastries, Navrátil — did you notice what time it closes?' he asked hopefully.

Unusually, Novák accepted Slonský's invitation to expound his findings over a coffee and a slab of poppyseed cake. Since the café in question was off the main tourist trail, the prices were only mildly extortionate, and for once Slonský had remembered his wallet, which was sure to burn the event securely into the memories of Navrátil and Novák.

'So, what do we have?' asked Slonský.

'Straightforward trauma caused by a blunt instrument,' answered Novák, 'and the pan we've sent for analysis could well have done the job.'

'The state of the flat suggests there wasn't a struggle,' Navrátil commented.

'No, but he wasn't killed where we found him,' Novák said. 'People who are hit like that don't lie nicely to attention on a rug. And given Vitek's penchant for tidiness, I think I can hazard a guess at what happened.'

Slonský put his cup down. 'Vitek was hit in the kitchen, then the rug was brought from the sitting room, Vitek was rolled onto it and the killer towed the rug back to the sitting room. But not being as tidy as Vitek, he didn't line it up parallel to the fireplace and sofa.'

'I was just going to say that,' grumbled Novák. 'It was my big moment.'

'I saved you the trouble. But you can comfort yourself with the knowledge that you were right.'

'Ah, but I have evidence. A couple of blood splashes in the kitchen. And the absence of any defensive wounds suggests that Vitek did not suspect what was coming.'

'Horrible way to go,' Slonský opined. 'One minute you're standing at the sink filling a kettle, and the next you're off to eternity with a hell of a headache. And done by someone who, apparently, was a friend.'

'How do you make that out?' asked Navrátil.

'He let them in. And he turned his back on them in the kitchen. If he'd suspected any kind of threat he wouldn't have done that.'

Navrátil fished in his pocket for his mobile phone and called up a photograph that he had taken. 'What do you make of that, sir?' he asked.

'It's a bookshelf, lad. Lots of houses have them. I don't, but then I'm not a big one for books.'

'Yes, sir, but look at the spines of the books.'

Slonský sighed dramatically and picked up the phone again. 'How do you go left and right on this thing?'

Navrátil showed him, so Slonský examined the length of the shelf. The sudden change in his expression demonstrated that he had realised the point that Navrátil had been trying to make.

'Oh, very good, lad!' He handed the phone to Novák, who glanced at it for no more than a second or two before handing it back.

'Sorted by authors' surnames, but R-Z is to the left, implying that the criminal lifted them off to look for something and didn't put them back correctly,' he said.

'How did you see that so quickly?' Slonský demanded to know. 'You're not even a trained detective.'

'Are you?' asked Novák.

'Self-taught,' proclaimed Slonský proudly. 'A graduate of the school of life.'

'Oh God, he's been reading the sweatshirts in Old Town Square again,' Novák murmured.

'All human life is there,' Slonský told him. 'I read somewhere that statistics show that everyone, at some time in their life, will come within five metres of a murderer. Personally, I've been handcuffed to a few, so I probably bias the results a bit.'

'I'm within five metres of you now,' said Novák, 'and if it wasn't for my Hippocratic Oath…'

Slonský snorted. 'I'm not worried about you. I've met some really evil, vicious scum in my time. Many of them hanging out in the police canteen. Then there were the ones we put behind bars. Remember that one we nabbed for peeing in the town hall mailbox?'

Novák's face assumed an expression of distaste. 'Only too well. I'd never had to forensically examine a pile of urine-soaked correspondence before.'

'Why did he do it?' asked Navrátil.

'God told him to, apparently,' Slonský replied. 'If you have as much experience of criminals being instructed by God to do things as I have, you're drawn to one of two conclusions. Either there are a lot of deluded people out there, or God is a sicko requiring some psychiatric help.'

'I know which way my vote is cast,' Navrátil replied primly.

'Ah yes, but that's because you and God have a chat every Sunday morning. Maybe you're biased. If I ever need to bring God in for questioning you'll have to recuse yourself, seeing as he's a mate.'

Navrátil refused to rise to the bait.

'You shouldn't tease him,' said Novák. 'It's good for a person to have something they passionately believe.'

'I know,' said Slonský. 'I have strong beliefs myself.'

'Really?' said Novák.

'Certainly. I strongly believe I'll have another piece of that cake.'

CHAPTER 2

There are people who can tell you exactly where they were when they heard that President Kennedy had been assassinated, or the Berlin Wall came down, or that Elvis Presley had died. Slonský would long remember where he was when this new bombshell hit.

He was at table seven in the police canteen, making short work of a ham sandwich, when Sergeant Mucha shook the very foundations of his belief system.

'I'm thinking of retiring after my birthday,' he said.

Slonský slapped the side of his own head.

'What did you do that for?' Mucha asked.

'Something's gone wrong with my hearing,' Slonský replied. 'I could have sworn you said that you were thinking of retiring.'

'I did.'

'Then maybe I should have slapped the side of *your* head,' Slonský retorted, 'to see if I could shock your brain back into life.'

'Somebody already did that,' remarked Mucha, gingerly rubbing the bruise on the top of his cheek. 'It's one of the reasons I'm thinking I've had enough.'

A few days before, a disgruntled service user had flung punches in all directions while being booked in at the front desk, one of which had landed squarely on Sergeant Mucha. A young officer had hit the panic alarm and, to give Colonel Rajka his credit, he had not hesitated. Despite being Director of the Criminal Police and therefore in a cosy office in the executive corridor, he had left his desk, run to the scene of disorder, sized up the situation at a glance and thrown the guilty party three metres across the floor before anyone else reacted. Rajka was a former Olympic Graeco-Roman wrestler and kept himself in good shape, so a mere ninety-kilo drunk was easy meat. He then pinioned the offender's arms until the cuffs could be applied.

'You've had worse,' Slonský opined.

'That doesn't make it sting any less,' Mucha pointed out. 'And I'm thinking here I am, nearly sixty, do I need this sort of aggravation? I could take my pension and sit at home doing my hobbies.'

'You don't have any hobbies.'

'That's not the point. I could get some. I could take up marquetry or learn to play the saxophone.'

'Isn't there enough misery in the world?'

'Thank you for your moral support.'

'You're welcome. I haven't even mentioned yet that being at home will subject you to more time in the company of the Evil Witch of Kutná Hora.'

Mucha shrugged. 'Maybe I've been too hard on my sister-in-law. She isn't that bad.'

'Then why have you worked two of the last three Christmas Days when you could have been at home with your wife and her family? After all, you draw up the roster.'

'Don't you dare tell my wife that.'

'Then don't go around spreading alarm and despondency by threatening to retire. If you go everyone will be pointing at me and wondering why I'm still here. And I'm eighteen months older than you.'

'Maybe it's time for you to go too. That knee thing you had last year was a warning.'

Slonský had damaged his knee ligaments trying to arrest a cat burglar called Pepa Mach. As the story developed through retelling, Mach was now as speedy as a gazelle, yet Slonský had managed to grab him at great cost to his knee, which had required two operations and a lot of rehabilitation. The clinic had given him a sheet of exercises to perform which he had followed diligently for nearly eight hours before deciding that going up and down the stairs to his flat, with a detour to the bar across the street, was at least as efficient a way of recovering his knee function.

'You've got a cruel tongue sometimes,' Slonský complained.

'Well, you're not as young as you were.'

'I'm younger than Major Lukas.'

'Yes, but he's got a nice desk job running internal investigations. A job which, I remind you, you could have had.'

'I don't want to be sitting at a desk.'

'Nobody ever ruptured a knee ligament sitting at a desk. Just saying.'

Slonský picked up his sandwich, took a large bite, and a jet of mustard shot straight down his shirt. 'Don't say a word,' he cautioned Mucha.

'Mucha? Retiring?' said Navrátil.

'That's what he says,' confirmed Slonský. 'We've got to stop him.'

'We?' asked Lieutenant Lucie Jerneková. 'Why we? He's your friend.'

'It's in all our interests to talk him out of it. If he retires we'll get someone new on the front desk.'

'Would that be so bad?' Jerneková persisted.

'Catastrophic! Mucha is the glue that keeps all the cogs turning.'

'I think you mean oil,' Navrátil replied. 'Or the glue that keeps us all together. But glueing cogs together is a bad idea.'

'Never mind what I mean,' Slonský retorted. 'The point is that it will bring about change, and in my experience change in the police service is rarely a good thing.'

'When I arrived,' Navrátil replied, 'you worked on your own.'

'Exactly my point.'

'And Captain Lukas was in your place, Rajka was head of internal investigations, Jerneková wasn't in the police, and Lieutenant Peiperová was working in Kladno. And I'd say all of the changes since then were for the best.'

'Yes, but it's been a lucky streak. It has to come to an end sometime. We can't go on being that fortunate. By the way, in case you hadn't noticed, you're married to Lieutenant Peiperová. You're allowed to use her first name.'

Navrátil looked very uncomfortable at the suggestion, as if Slonský had proposed that he should do something highly improper like sharing a coffee spoon with her in public.

'They might give the job to Sergeant Salzer,' Officer Krob chipped in. 'You get on all right with him.'

Salzer was Mucha's deputy and often worked the night shift. He was in his forties, built like a sentry box and notoriously taciturn. This brooding moodiness was much appreciated by Slonský, who liked to have Salzer in the room when he was interrogating people because the silent goliath somehow transmitted the idea that, left to his own devices, he would be pounding a confession out of the suspect.

'I doubt it would be Salzer,' Slonský said, shaking his head. 'He hasn't been cleared on that assault inquiry yet.'

This was a reference to the odd incident of the teacher who was found in the back of his car with a half-naked boy in the woods near Dejvice and who somehow broke three fingers while signing his confession. Salzer claimed not to have seen anything, which may well have been true, since he had closed his eyes. Krob, who had been taking the confession, could hardly have done it because his shoulder was still paining him after a suspect tried to evade arrest by jumping off a hillside while handcuffed to him. Krob had managed to grab a tree to save himself. In any event, Krob had left the room to wash his hands, having handled some of the exhibits in the case.

'Didn't Sergeant Salzer say that the suspect jammed his own hand in a desk drawer?' Jerneková commented.

'Not exactly,' Slonský replied. 'As usual, he's saying nothing. That was a suggestion made by one of Major Lukas' team at the inquiry that Salzer didn't contradict.'

'It's not very likely though, is it?' said Navrátil. 'Why would a suspect deliberately injure himself and blame a police officer?'

'So he can blame a police officer,' Slonský answered. 'You'd be surprised how many I've known who have done something to themselves so they can claim we forced a confession out of them. You've seen it yourself. What about that fellow who banged his head on the desk when we were questioning him?'

'Only because you pulled his chair away.'

'I noticed it had a wobbly leg. I didn't want him tipping sideways and hurting himself. Anyway, stop being negative and do something to help me for once. How are we going to persuade Mucha not to hand his notice in?'

'Salzer could break three of his fingers so he can't write,' Jerneková said.

'We need to formulate a plan of action,' said Slonský, ignoring her suggestion but filing it away mentally as a last resort. 'Now, where do we start?'

*

Slonský's friend and confidant, journalist Mr Valentin, was no more help when Slonský laid the problem before him that evening.

'Are police pensions that good?' he enquired.

'I don't know. I haven't had mine yet,' Slonský replied. 'But we're not trying to justify his decision to leave, we're trying to find ways of talking him out of it. Any ideas?'

'No.'

'Couldn't you lie a bit to cheer me up?'

'No, I've had a lifelong devotion to the truth.'

'Then why did you become a journalist? You won't fit in with that attitude.'

'I shall ignore that snide remark. It was unworthy of you.'

'Put it down to the balance of my mind being disturbed. I've got to find a conclusive argument that stops Mucha going.'

'Have you played the sister-in-law card?' Valentin asked.

'Right at the start.'

'And it didn't change his mind?'

'No. He thinks he may have misjudged her all these years.'

'Goodness! How hard was that bang on the head he took?'

'There's a thought. I could try to persuade the personnel department that he can't make rational decisions due to his head injury.'

'Wouldn't they just turf him out anyway? I'd have thought a lack of mental capacity would be a major handicap to a police officer.'

'At our level, perhaps. But in the executive corridor it could be a positive advantage.'

Valentin took a sip of pear brandy and considered the matter. 'Maybe the answer is not to do with telling him how awful he'll find retirement. Maybe you need to concentrate on how much he'll miss work.'

'The trouble is that he won't. Nobody misses being clonked on the cranium by drunks.'

'But what about his sense of achievement? Perhaps he needs a big win to satisfy his ego.'

'Mucha? Achievement? He's a desk sergeant. What kind of achievement can he have?'

'Hang on — you've told me in the past that his help has been invaluable.'

'Yes, when we wanted some old file tracked down. He's a wizard at hunting out old folders that haven't been digitised yet.'

'Digitised?'

'There's a scheme under which we pay students and other derelicts to scan all the old files into the computer. Don't ask me how it works. But it means we can get rid of a mountain of paper and clever people like Navrátil can find things inside those digitised files. I have no idea how, but it saves a lot of time. Of course, paying people to do all that is expensive, and the money ran out years ago, so we're still reliant on paper files, and only old codgers like Mucha can remember the filing system or have any idea where files might be kept. Only last year he remembered that there was a warehouse near the airport that might have something useful in it, and he was right.'

'So send him to get files. It doesn't matter if you don't actually use them, so long as he gets the satisfaction of finding them.'

'He's not that shallow. He'd ask me what we did with the information, and I can't pull the wool over his eyes.'

'Why not? You pull it over everyone else's.'

*

It was a measure of the desperation that Slonský was feeling that he found himself tiptoeing along the executive corridor in police headquarters trying hard not to look as if he was heading for a disciplinary hearing. Rather, he was bound for the last set of rooms on the left. Bypassing the penultimate room where the lower grades sat, he knocked on the door of the last office.

'Come!' announced a familiar voice.

Slonský opened the door, quickly glancing behind himself to check that nobody he knew was watching him.

'Slonský! Whatever brings you here?' asked Major Lukas, then, sensing that this may have appeared less than friendly he added, 'Not that you're not welcome, of course.'

'I was hoping for some guidance, sir,' Slonský said.

'You don't have to whisper. Everything said here is confidential and there is nobody to overhear.'

'No, sir.'

Lukas put down his pen and leaned back in his chair. 'I'm not accustomed to being asked for advice by you, Slonský.'

'I don't like to burden you when you already have such arduous responsibilities,' Slonský replied.

'Not too arduous at present in the Office of Internal Investigations. I'm pleased to say that corruption in the police service is down twelve per cent over the last year.'

Under normal circumstances Slonský might have questioned how anyone could assert that, given that corrupt police do not normally announce the fact, but he let it slide this time. It probably meant that corrupt police had become twelve per cent more cunning at hiding what they were up to. It also helped that the organised crime division was so inept that criminals didn't even need to bribe them to escape capture.

'I'm pleased to hear that, sir. I know how much you detest corruption.'

That much was true. Slonský had known Lukas for over thirty years and there was no doubt that Lukas' promotion had been seriously delayed under the old regime because of his refusal to act unethically. After all, if senior officers are on the take they need to know that their immediate deputies are similarly tainted or they would not sleep at night.

'I can't claim all the credit. Colonel Rajka had made significant inroads before me.'

'Nevertheless, even small advances are worth having.'

'Yes. Now, what did you want to ask me?'

'Sergeant Mucha is thinking of retiring.'

To Slonský's gratification, this news so startled Lukas that he jerked forward and almost overturned his chair. 'Good heavens! Are you sure?'

'He said so only yesterday.'

Lukas looked exceptionally perturbed. 'This is extremely worrying. Mucha is a model officer and a great example to the young men under his wing.'

'And women, sir.'

'Quite. Are there any women under Mucha's wing?'

'No. But if there were, he would be a great example to them.'

'Oh, certainly. It goes without saying. But what are we going to do to persuade him to reconsider?'

'I don't know, sir. That's why I came to you.'

Lukas shook his head sadly. 'I confess to being at something of a loss. It is clearly vital that we convince him that he is needed, but I am not sure how. I shall have to give the matter some thought.'

'I would be grateful, sir,' Slonský said, and he meant it.

'Everything else in order?' Lukas asked. 'My old team still performing?'

'It certainly is.'

'I always thought Navrátil had something about him.'

'A first-rate detective, sir.'

'And that woman you brought from Kladno — Peiperová. Quite a find. You did well there, Josef.'

So we're on first name terms again? That's good, thought Slonský.

'And those two new officers you've recruited — how are they doing?'

'Krob is a calm and efficient officer, sir. Exactly the sort of man you liked to have. Never flustered. And Jerneková will be very good once she has completed her training. She has an imaginative way of working.'

By imaginative Slonský really meant off the wall, but Lukas took the remark at face value. Jerneková would be much more useful once she has a driver's licence, thought Slonský, if indeed she ever achieved a driver's licence, which was looking a little less likely since she had driven a police car through a market when she responded to a call while halfway through a lesson. Colonel Rajka had begun to mumble that a driving qualification was not absolutely mandatory for all detectives and had made clear that he would not, in future, cover the cost of damaged property from the departmental budget. Slonský had made general enquiries about the availability of a police bicycle, though he doubted whether Jerneková's diminutive legs would make cycling a viable option. There was no doubt that she was very keen to learn to drive, and she spent every spare hour pestering the driving school to give her more practice, but given that one instructor was now off work with a stress-related illness the school regretted that opportunities would be limited.

Slonský's route back to his office took him past the front desk. Mucha looked up and smiled at him. Slonský could not even summon up a few words of friendly abuse in reply.

CHAPTER 3

Lieutenant Kristýna Peiperová signed the paperwork and pushed it back over the counter to Mucha.

'Is that it?' he asked. 'Only if you arrest any more ticket inspectors they'll have to sleep standing up.'

'I think that's it. You've got a few cells there and I only booked eight of them.'

'Jerneková brought a couple in while you were in the ladies' toilet. If it's a quiet evening Salzer can move a few around, but we need to keep a couple of cells free for anyone brought in during the night.'

'I'm sure you'll cope,' said Peiperová and flashed him the sort of smile that ensured that he would do anything she asked. For a moment he felt quite jealous of Navrátil.

'I'll see what we can do.'

'Where is Lucie anyway?' Peiperová asked.

'Gone up to the office, I think.'

'It's high time she went back to the barracks and got some rest. And the same goes for you.'

'I haven't lived in the barracks for years. And never in the women's ones.'

'You know what I mean. Your wife will be waiting for you. She's probably got you a lovely supper ready.'

'Only if she's invited her sister over again and wants to butter me up.'

'Just think — if you were retired you could have the pleasure of your sister-in-law's company all day.'

Mucha closed his day-book with a resounding thump. 'Don't bother. Your boss has already tried that line on me and he's much more devious than you.'

Peiperová bounded up the stairs in search of her assistant, whom she found at her desk. Jerneková was lounging back in her chair with her feet on the desk, a jar of pickles on her lap and a cat's cradle of coloured wool tangled around her.

'What are you doing?' Peiperová asked.

'It's all part of my plan to get Sergeant Mucha to stay,' Jerneková explained.

'How? Are you going to tie him up?'

'No. I'm knitting him a pair of socks to show how much we appreciate him.'

'I didn't know you could knit.'

'I can't, but it can't be that difficult. I've been watching videos on the internet.'

'On a police computer?'

Jerneková shrugged. 'Why not? The socks are going on police feet.'

Dr Novák held out the pot of menthol ointment, into which Navrátil gratefully dipped a finger to transfer some to his top lip. Slonský seemed not to be affected by the smell and had to be encouraged to stand a little further back to allow Novák to walk freely around the mortuary table.

'An interesting case,' Novák announced, as if the two detectives were students. 'First, my suspicions were correct. There's a very large bleed just above the right ear, caused by a deep depression in the skull where it was hit with a blunt object.'

Slonský leaned forward and peered at the body. 'I can see that. I don't suppose the maker's name was imprinted into the skin or anything useful like that?'

'Unfortunately not. The object was so large that I can't tell you whether the assailant was taller or shorter. I suspect the victim was standing because there is quite typical *coup-contrecoup* pathology.'

'You'll have to explain that for the lad,' said Slonský.

'Why don't you explain it?' Novák replied.

'I'd prefer you to do it,' Slonský said, 'in case my explanation is too technical for him.'

Novák grabbed a teaching model of a head from a shelf and pointed to each temple in turn. 'Right side, left side,' he said.

'I think we've got that,' Slonský commented. 'Do you need to make a note, lad?'

Novák growled a little under his breath. 'When a head is hit, you get a coup injury, from a French word meaning to hit or strike. But if the head then hits something solid, you get a contrecoup injury, when the brain moves within the skull and is hammered against the skull on the opposite side to the contact.'

Navrátil frowned. 'If the original blow is on the right, and Vitek falls over and bangs his head, he'll hit the left side, meaning the contrecoup injury for that second contact would be on the right, so how can you tell the coup from the contrecoup?'

'A very good question, Navrátil,' Slonský interjected. 'I was just going to ask that.'

'Because,' Novák explained, 'the head is unlikely to be hit exactly square, so when the far side hits a wall or floor it's going to cause a rebound injury that doesn't exactly coincide with the original. In this case, if you look at Vitek's head, slightly in front of his left ear you'll see a dent. And in those photos of the crime scene on the cork board behind you there is a drawer handle that matches the dent very well. The original blow seems to be centred just above but slightly behind the right ear, whereas the dent is at the same height but about two and a half centimetres further forward. And the contrecoup damage to that is where we would expect it.'

'Would he have died instantly?' Navrátil asked.

'No, but he doesn't seem to have tried to move much, so I suspect he was knocked out by the blow. The skull fragments ripped into an artery and blood started to spurt out. Some went under the soft tissues and caused that uneven look we commented on, while some went into the brain. With three-quarters of a litre of blood passing through the brain every minute it wouldn't take long for the pressure to cause catastrophic brain damage. With prompt medical attention he might have survived but without it he would have died quite quickly, I think.'

'Presumably,' Slonský suggested, 'he was dead when the killer left the flat? Why move someone who is still alive? And if the killer wanted him dead wouldn't you give him a couple of extra thumps just to make sure?'

'I bow to your knowledge of what goes on in a criminal's head,' Novák retorted. 'I stick to what goes on in the victim's head.'

'The thing is,' Slonský rejoined, 'nothing much goes on in a criminal's head. That's why they're criminals. If they stopped to think, they'd realise I'll catch them and they wouldn't do it.'

'There must be some criminals you haven't caught,' Navrátil claimed.

'Of course,' said Slonský. 'I have to leave one or two for you. You can have first dibs on this one if you like.'

'I seem to remember that the last time I led on a case you took it back off me.'

'I don't remember that. I just gave a bit of supervisory guidance, that's all.'

'So this case is really mine?'

'Yes. Do you want it in writing?'

'No. Your word is good enough for me, sir.'

'You haven't had a bang on the head, too?' Novák asked Navrátil.

Navrátil and Krob opened the door and stepped into Vitek's flat. Although they knew that the owner was currently in a chiller cabinet some kilometres away it still seemed rather intrusive of them, even though they were wearing plastic covers on their shoes.

Krob looked at the bookshelves. 'So we're assuming that the killer believed that something was hidden here and took the time to look for it, then tried to conceal the fact by putting everything back neatly, but put one armful back in the wrong place?'

'That's about it,' Navrátil confirmed.

'So we don't know whether the killer found the unknown item that we're looking for?'

'That's about it too.'

Krob looked carefully at the photograph Navrátil had given him. 'Well, they're still in the order you found, so let's assume that R to Z is one armful and take those off first.' Suiting action to the word, he reached forward and lifted an armful of books from the third shelf. Looking around for a convenient surface he stacked them vertically on a coffee table. 'Then we're left with about double the number of books I've just removed, so let's lift off half of what's left.'

'Put them on the desk here,' Navrátil suggested.

There was no sign of anything behind them, so Krob proceeded to lift off the last batch of books, and carefully transported them to the desk too.

'Well, I'll be…' Navrátil exclaimed, his mouth dropping open. Krob turned to look at whatever had caught Navrátil's attention. There was a small safe in the corner of the shelf.

'It's cemented to the brick wall on this side,' Navrátil commented. 'And there's a metal bar in front to stop anyone easily pulling the whole thing out.'

'Where does the bar go?' asked Krob.

'Around the safe above the door and into a pillar behind. Let's take a look in the adjoining room to see if we can get to the back of it.'

The detectives walked through but were met with a blank wall.

'Just a moment,' Krob remarked. 'Look at the floorboards.'

Navrátil glanced down, but Krob had already dropped to his knees.

'These are newer than the others,' he said, before suddenly leaving the flat. After a few minutes he returned looking triumphant. 'I've been measuring up the floors below,' he explained. 'Each has a cupboard in this room, but Vitek robbed it to create an alcove for his safe. And the problem of living in a flat is finding something solid enough to stop thieves just lifting out your safe and taking it away, but it looks as if Vitek had at least one of the floorboard joists replaced or augmented with a steel girder. The woman below remembers the noise when it was put in.'

'So whatever is in that safe, Vitek wanted it to stay there.'

'Evidently.'

Now it was Navrátil's turn to run through to the study once more. 'Look — it's a double decker safe. Here's a larger compartment behind this false panel.'

'So even if you spotted the top compartment, you might not know that there was a second compartment below.'

'To be honest, the false panel didn't take much spotting, once you suspected that there would be no point in a steel girder beneath unless the safe was connected to it somehow.'

Krob scratched his head. 'So what do we do now?'

Navrátil needed no thought. 'We see if Spehar and his team of technicians can get into it.'

'No need for that!' Slonský declared. 'You already know a better answer.'

'Better?' said Navrátil.

'Well, involving less paperwork. That's always better in my book.'

Navrátil thought briefly. 'You're not suggesting Mr Fingers?' he asked.

'I am indeed suggesting Mr Fingers,' Slonský replied. 'If he can't open it, it can't be opened.'

'Who is Mr Fingers?' Krob enquired.

'He's a freelance security consultant,' Slonský explained.

'Who just happens to be an old thief,' added Navrátil.

'Who has seen the error of his way and gone straight,' Slonský replied. 'He now uses his considerable experience to explain to people how they can avoid being burgled by the likes of him.'

'Does he get much business with a name like Mr Fingers?' Krob asked.

'That's not his real name, obviously,' Slonský said. 'His real name is … something else. Can't remember at the moment.

Mucha will know if you're that bothered. The point is that he's good. Navrátil can vouch for him.'

'He burglar-proofed our flat when we got married,' Navrátil said. 'It was the boss's wedding present to us.'

'And have you been burgled since?' Slonský asked.

'No,' conceded Navrátil. 'It takes us about five minutes to get in when we arrive home but it's certainly secure.'

'I rest my case,' said Slonský. 'I'll give him a ring while you rustle up some coffees for the journey.'

'What journey?' Navrátil wanted to know.

'The journey to Vitek's flat. You can't just let Mr Fingers wander round in there unsupervised, you know. The man's got a criminal record as long as your arm.'

CHAPTER 4

Peiperová gritted her teeth. Sometimes a woman just has to do what a woman has to do, she thought. No point being wimpy about it. She lobbed the car keys to Jerneková. 'Right, it's all yours. I know we're off road but try not to hit anything. And take it easy, please. I don't want to have to explain any more dents in cars.'

Jerneková reddened. Whether it was with the excitement of being entrusted with a car or the injustice of being blamed for the incident with the deer was not clear. 'I'll do my best,' she exclaimed.

'You'll do it perfectly and safely,' Peiperová said sternly, 'or you'll be reliving the Forties, when police went everywhere by tram.'

'Yes, boss. Ma'am. Kristýna.'

They clambered into the car and Jerneková started the engine, which Peiperová promptly reached over to switch off.

'Seat belt first, Lucie.'

Jerneková grabbed the buckle, clipped it in place, then shuffled from side to side until the strap nestled properly in her cleavage. 'You can tell seat belts were invented by a bloke who didn't have these to contend with,' she grumbled.

'Maybe, but it'll keep you safe.'

'Little children have harnesses with straps that go between your legs. You'll notice the bloke who invented these didn't go down that route. I wonder why?' Jerneková said primly.

She started the engine, ostentatiously checked her rear-view mirror, and drove off along the track. Presumably there were some gears engaged between first and fourth, but if so their participation was very fleeting.

'This is great,' Jerneková enthused. 'When I've got my licence I'll feel like I'm part of the team.'

'You're already part of the team,' Peiperová replied. 'A very important part.'

'Yeah, but I'm a passenger. You lot have to take me everywhere.'

'If you don't slow for the bend I'll be taking you to hospital.'

Jerneková eased her foot off the accelerator, an action somewhat negated by her shift to a lower gear and her exuberant turning of the steering wheel. 'I envy you,' she said unexpectedly.

'Me? Why?'

'You're living the dream, aren't you? Good husband, earning good money, got your own place to live. It's not just you. I envy Krob too. He's got a smashing wife, two lovely kids.'

'Are you getting broody?' Peiperová asked with a teasing smile.

'Why do you say that?'

'A little bird tells me you've been babysitting for Krob and his wife.'

'He promised not to tell!'

'He didn't. His wife rang the other day to tell him to tell you that she was held up so not to dash over there, but since he wasn't in the office I took the message. She obviously thought I knew already.'

'Oh. Well, got to get a man first, haven't I? It's just that biological clock thing.'

'Lucie, you're still young.'

'Yeah, but I read this thing in some women's magazine that said your fertility goes down stupid per cent every year after you're thirty.'

'Take your time, Lucie.'

'I'm not getting any younger…'

'I meant on the road, now. If you don't accelerate so hard down the straight you won't need to brake so much at the bend.'

'That's the best bit.'

'Maybe, but it's not the safest. When you get to the end I want you to stop and reverse into that garage.'

'Reverse? I haven't done reversing.'

'You will now. Just take it slowly. Anyway, I thought you said you weren't that bothered about men?'

'I'm not. Most of them are a waste of space. But until women grow balls we need them for some things, don't we?'

'This is going to take some explaining,' Jerneková said ten minutes later.

'I think we've got them,' Peiperová replied. 'Thank goodness they all survived.'

'You never said someone was keeping chickens in the garage,' said Jerneková accusingly.

'I didn't know or I wouldn't have asked you to reverse into it, would I?'

'The car's barely marked,' Jerneková claimed, spitting on a handkerchief and attempting to polish out a scratch on the rear bumper.

'Shame we can't say the same for the fencing. Give me a hand to pick up that post you snapped.'

'*We* snapped. I'm not taking all the blame. I was following a legitimate order given by my superior officer.'

'Never mind that. Let's get it upright and see if it can be fixed.'

Jerneková was rummaging on a workbench at the back of the garage before advancing with a hammer in her hand and a couple of fifteen-centimetre nails. 'These should hold it,' she said, hammering one in from each side. 'There — good as new.'

Peiperová looked doubtful. 'You don't think the tilt gives it away?'

'It'll keep the chickens in. Now, let's get out of here before anyone asks us awkward questions.'

They climbed back into the car and Jerneková drove it carefully along the road towards the exit.

'Don't look now,' she muttered, 'but we've got a passenger on the back seat.'

'Did you know someone was keeping chickens in the garage?' Peiperová demanded on their return.

'No, or I'd have told them not to keep chickens in the garage,' said the driving school superintendent.

'I think they may have knocked over one of the fence posts,' Jerneková added.

'Did they now?' said the superintendent, not without a measure of suspicion, but it does not do to accuse police officers of lying to you.

'We'll say no more about it,' said Jerneková. 'We don't police wildlife permits.'

'Since when have chickens been wildlife?' asked the superintendent. 'I thought that was all about lions and wolves.'

'Them as well,' Jerneková conceded. 'But I didn't see any of them in the garage.'

'I'm glad to hear it.'

Peiperová signed them both out in the register and handed over the car keys. 'Thanks. By the way, there's a chicken on the back seat. We thought it was best not to let her out on the track.'

'Very considerate of you, I'm sure.'

Navrátil, Krob and Slonský were in Vitek's flat waiting for the arrival of Mr Fingers. Suddenly he was in the room with them.

'Didn't you lock the front door?' Navrátil demanded.

'I'm sure I did,' Krob replied.

'He did, but it's child's play,' Mr Fingers announced. 'Now, where's this safe?'

Navrátil removed the concealing panel to show the lower door, the upper door already being on view.

'Oh ho! A custom-made one. Your friend didn't mind splashing out a bit. Shame he didn't ask me, I could have got it done at wholesale prices.'

'You don't know how much he paid,' Slonský pointed out.

'Whatever it was, I'm cheaper,' Mr Fingers told them cheerily. 'Now, let's see. Electronic keypads. You'll want to stand back, gentlemen.'

'Are you going to blow it open?' Navrátil asked, already striding towards the hallway.

'No, I'm going to use this,' Mr Fingers answered, reaching into his bag and brandishing a thick piece of brown material.

'A hiking sock?' asked Slonský.

'Not exactly. There's a magnet inside. Don't come near me if you've got a mobile phone.'

He slapped the sock against the safe, moved it a little and then turned the handle and it sprang open. He then repeated the action on the upper part.

'There you go. All those complicated wires and things, but in the end something has to make the locks spring in and out, and a magnet does it just as well.'

'I could have done that,' Slonský protested.

'Yes,' conceded Mr Fingers, 'if you had a lifetime's experience telling you where to stick the magnet.'

'Oh, I could tell you where to stick the magnet,' Slonský replied, but peeled off a couple of banknotes and handed them over.

'Do you want a receipt?'

'What would you do if I said yes?'

'Kick the safe door shut and invite you to open it again with your own sock.'

'Where does the sock come into it?'

Mr Fingers grinned. 'If I didn't have a sock to pull on, I'd never get the magnet back off the door. Well, I can't stand around all day yakking. I've got a living to make.'

'You just made a couple of thousand crowns for ten seconds' work,' Slonský pointed out.

'I've got overheads to meet. Transport, taxes, tools of the trade.' He held up the sock again. 'These aren't cheap, you know. No need to show me to the door. I'll see myself out.' He lowered his voice to murmur to Slonský. 'If you want that front door making secure, tip me the wink. I could do with getting on the list for police work.'

Slonský patted him on the shoulder. 'I trust you, but the police have funny rules about employing people with criminal records.'

'I've paid my debt to society. I thought the police of all people would expect a man to make an honest living.'

'You obviously haven't met some of my senior colleagues. I'll do what I can for you.'

'You're a good man, Captain Slonský. I bless the day I got nicked by you.'

'Was that the fourth, fifth or sixth time?'

Mr Fingers grinned again and shut the door behind him.

Slonský inspected each folder from the top safe in turn before handing it to Navrátil.

'He's very tidy,' Slonský said. 'Mucha would be proud of this standard of filing.'

'What do you make of it, sir?'

'If I find a bundle of folders in a safe with a person's name on the front and cryptic notes inside I would tend to think blackmail may be involved, wouldn't you?'

'Blackmail?'

'Well, take this one. Maria Suková. Here we've got a couple of photographs of a woman chatting to a man in what looks like a hotel lobby, and one of them walking together towards the elevators. And a photocopy of a receipt.'

'But look at the date, sir,' said Krob. 'Twelfth of May, 1986. It's not exactly current. Can anything this old really be blackmail material?'

'I suppose that depends on who these people are. If Ms Suková is married and this man isn't her husband that could still be a problem for her, couldn't it?'

'They're just walking towards a lift, sir,' Navrátil pointed out.

'Ah, there you go, lad, seeing the good side of everybody again. If you were like me and started with the assumption that everyone is up to something you'd solve a lot more crime. They may just be walking towards a lift, Navrátil, but I doubt they're just going up to an upper floor for the ride. Well, not that kind of ride, anyway.'

'That's a big assumption based on one photograph, sir.'

'Three photographs, lad. And look at the twinkle in her eye in this one. If a woman ever looks at you like that cross your legs and check your zip is fully up. Except your wife, I suppose.'

Krob had picked up each folder from the upper safe in turn. 'Sir, I think all of these are women.'

'Are they now? That's interesting. Tell you what — you take these back to the office and make me a nice chart of their names, addresses, dates of birth, jobs; in fact, anything you can glean from them. Have you looked in the lower safe yet?'

Navrátil crouched to pull the folders from the lower safe. As he yanked the pile forward there was an explosion and the room filled with black smoke. Navrátil and Krob groped blindly for the door, guided by Slonský's calls.

'Are you all right?'

Navrátil coughed and retched. 'Not too good,' he admitted. 'But I'm breathing, and I'm unharmed.'

'You're also purple,' Krob pointed out. 'At least your hands and front are. And so are those folders.'

'Let's get that off and get the technicians up here,' Slonský said.

Technician First Class Spehar, normally an even-tempered man, was frowning and a little snappy. 'I don't know why you didn't send for us to open the safe in the first place,' he muttered.

'It didn't go bang when it was opened,' Slonský explained. 'It went off when Navrátil took these folders out.'

'I know,' said Spehar. 'A rookie mistake. Thank goodness whoever set it up didn't put a serious amount of explosive in there. Look, this bottom folder, the dark green one, has a wire leading from its top edge. It never had anything useful in it. Its whole purpose was to stay in the safe. Vitek must have known that, so he would never try to take it out. Anyone who did would yank on the wire and trigger the dye explosion. The banks use the same method to safeguard banknotes in transit.'

'Navrátil would be very glad of any advice you could give on getting the purple dye off his hands. Children are calling him names in the street.'

'Well, if he finds a way, perhaps he'd let me know. It's indelible. That's the whole point of it.'

'You mean he'll stay purple for ever?'

'Not for ever. Few weeks, perhaps. The skin renews itself about every three weeks so he'll begin to fade quite quickly.'

Navrátil was sitting gazing at his hands, mute but despairing. He looked so miserable that Spehar began to soften.

'The dyes are usually anthraquinones. They don't dissolve in water or room-temperature solvents, but hot alcohol sometimes makes an impression.'

'Hot wine? I know a kiosk that sells that,' Slonský announced, brightening immediately.

'Not at this time of year, sir,' Navrátil moaned.

'At all times of year, lad, if you know where to look.'

'There's no need for that,' said Spehar. 'Besides, the proportion of alcohol in hot wine isn't going to make much difference.' He produced a small bottle from his case. 'Can you get me a cup of hot water?' he asked.

'Krob, be a good fellow and ask Dumpy Anna in the canteen if she can give Navrátil a cup of hot water,' ordered Slonský.

Krob returned within a few minutes with the cup. 'She said since it's for Navrátil there's no charge,' he said.

'Really?' replied Slonský. 'I must send Navrátil down to get my lunch more often.'

Spehar loosened the cap of the bottle and stood it in the cup.

'What happens now?' demanded Slonský. 'Does it turn pink or something?'

'Patience, Captain, patience. I'm waiting for it to warm up.'

'Can't we just light a match under it?'

'Only if you don't like having an office. Think of it as a variant on petrol and then decide whether you want to strike a match near it.'

Slonský scratched his head. 'I knew a taxi driver once, Pospišil by name. Always wore a fur hunter's cap, winter or summer. He was a compulsive chain-smoker. Never seen without a cigarette hanging out of his mouth, and we used to tell him one day he'd be filling up his taxi and he'd blow the thing up.'

'And did he?' asked Spehar.

'Sort of. He dropped the cigarette in his lap one day when he was driving and while he looked down to find it he didn't notice a monster truck coming towards him. Very nasty.'

'And the point of that story was…?'

'No particular point. Just an observation on the rich tapestry of life.'

Spehar declared himself satisfied with the temperature of the solvent, selected a long-handled cotton swab from his kit and dipped it in the liquid, applying it to the back of Navrátil's hand. Navrátil flinched and said something.

'I'm surprised at you knowing a word like that,' said Slonský, 'and you an ardent churchgoer.'

'Sorry. It's rather hot.'

'It needs to be or the dye won't dissolve,' Spehar explained. 'As hot as you can bear it.'

It was at this moment that Peiperová and Jerneková walked in.

'What's happened?' a concerned Peiperová demanded of her husband.

'It's a long story. I've been dyed.'

'I can see that. Will it come off?'

'That's what Technician Spehar is trying to find out.'

'Looks like you'll be sleeping in the spare room tonight,' Jerneková proclaimed. 'There's no way you'll be allowed to get that on the Egyptian cotton sheets.'

'How do you know they've got Egyptian cotton sheets on their bed?' Slonský asked Jerneková. If it was intended to be asked discreetly, it was a failure, because everyone turned to look at her as she answered.

'Because it was on their wedding present list. I gave them the matching pillowcases.'

'Ah, I see.'

'Did you think I'd been rolling around on their bed with one of them?' Jerneková enquired.

'Not at all,' stammered Slonský. 'Just idle curiosity.'

Spehar broke the tension by holding his swab aloft. 'Have you got a waste bin?' he asked.

Krob quickly produced one from the side of his desk.

'It's coming off bit by bit,' said Spehar. 'It's going to be a long job and it'll dry his skin out if I do this for too long. I'll send a bottle over when I get back to the lab. Just keep at it a few minutes at a time with the hot solvent. Best wear gloves yourself,' he warned Peiperová. 'You don't want to transfer the dye to your hands.'

Peiperová nodded her understanding.

'I'll take the folders and see if we can make anything of their contents,' Spehar announced. 'I'll keep you posted.'

'Thank you,' said Slonský, 'from me and the Oompa-Loompa there.'

'Weren't the Oompa-Loompas orange?' commented Jerneková.

'Orange, purple, what's the difference?'

'Well, if you're orange, you'll think orange is normal, and you won't want to be purple,' Jerneková explained. 'They taught us that in our unconscious racial bias awareness training.'

Slonský sighed. 'If we ever arrest an Oompa-Loompa I promise not to let his orange colour lead me to discriminate against him.'

'Or her,' Jerneková added.

'Or her,' Slonský agreed. 'Now, can we get back to work?'

'Let's get some coffee,' said Jerneková breezily, who wanted to ensure that the opportunity to discuss any recent driving lessons that she might have had did not arise, and she marched out of the room, closely followed by Slonský.

CHAPTER 5

By the following morning the purple discolouration of Navrátil's skin had, after a couple of showers and the application of a number of highly-fragranced women's cosmetic creams, faded to a rather fetching deep pink, though it was now clear that the dye had struck the front of his hair and the tip of his nose.

'I'm not sure it wasn't better when you were purple,' Slonský commented. 'At least then it looked a bit like a bruise.'

'I'd better complete an accident report,' Navrátil replied.

'Why? It wasn't an accident, was it? You meant to lift the folders out. A deliberate act can't be an accident.'

'I didn't know it was going to explode, though. It could have been a lot more serious than it was.'

'I'll give you that,' Slonský agreed. 'It's a good thing you looked up at Krob or you'd have taken it full in the face.'

'You're all treating this as a bit of a joke,' Navrátil complained. 'It's a serious matter.'

'It's gallows humour,' Slonský explained. 'Endemic in the police service. You should have heard what folks said to me when I got a bullet in my rear end. Have I ever told you that one?'

'Many times,' Navrátil told him, 'or at least the nub of the story. But you've never explained where and when it happened.'

Slonský plonked his feet up on the desk. You can't tell a good story when you're uncomfortable. 'It was back in the mid-eighties — 1985, if I remember correctly. A lovely spring morning. The flowers were poking through, the birds were singing, and all was quiet except for the occasional little patter of small arms fire. Lukas and I were summoned to a warehouse in Libeň. Some of our fellows had interrupted a bit of private enterprise being conducted there, and it had turned nasty. The officer in charge decided we would storm all the doors simultaneously, on the grounds that they couldn't shoot us all. I think it's the only time Mucha ever held a door open for me. "After you," he said, so I piled in and knelt down behind some pallets. Unfortunately, they spotted Mucha and took a shot at him. He had dived full length and it missed him, but he was a sitting duck. Or, more accurately, a lying one. So I stood up and fired a couple of shots off, then I thought I'd better get behind something a bit more substantial than a pile of wood, so I ran behind a steel pillar. I was slimmer in those days, you understand. Anyway, Mucha got into some cover and the bullets started flying again, and I was just feeling really good about the fact that they were hitting the wall behind me when a ricochet got me.'

'Where were you shot?' Krob asked.

'I told you, right behind the pillar. Hurt like billy-o. I lost interest in things for a few minutes, but my colleagues dealt with the bad guys and Mucha came over to give me first aid.'

'That was good of him,' Navrátil said.

'He took one look at the wound and said, "If that gets infected I'm not sucking the poison out." Selfish beggar. I wouldn't mind but they tried to charge me for a new pair of uniform trousers.' Slonský rose to his feet and gently kneaded his backside. 'Still get a twinge when the weather's changing.'

'It'll be stinging a bit today then. I think there's a storm brewing.'

'You could be right, lad.'

Slonský stood by the window, and Navrátil thought he could see a tear forming in Slonský's eye.

'It's quite an emotional story, sir.'

'I've often thought that if Mucha got shot I'd do the same for him. Or not, depending on where the wound was, of course. And now I won't get the chance.' He turned abruptly with a renewed sense of purpose. 'He can't retire, Navrátil. It's time to put a stop to this foolishness. Operation End of the World is about to start.'

'Let it go,' pleaded Valentin.

'I can't,' Slonský replied. 'The man doesn't know what's good for him.'

'In what sense can putting up with you for a day longer than he has to be described as "good for him"?'

'In the sense that we've worked together for forty years. Two-thirds of my life has been spent with Mucha. That's about twenty times longer than I was married.'

'You're still married,' Valentin snapped back, and immediately wished he had not. It was an insensitive thing to say.

'Technically, perhaps; but I haven't had to live with her since 1970.'

Slonský's ex-wife had admitted a little while before that she had never actually filed their divorce papers.

'Věra made a mistake. She tried to make amends,' Valentin suggested.

'By conveniently forgetting to tell me she'd been living with someone else for a couple of years? Anyway, we're getting off the point. Mucha is deserting me and we have to stop him.'

'If you'd tried to stop Věra from leaving what would you have done?'

Slonský thought for a moment. 'I don't think a bunch of flowers and a quickie on the kitchen table is going to work with Mucha. But if you think it would, I'm desperate enough to try anything.'

Valentin pinched his nose until it hurt. It temporarily blanked out the image in his brain. 'The general principle holds true. Show him he's appreciated. I know it goes against the grain, but say something nice to him every day.'

'Something nice? To Mucha?'

'Yes. Give it a go. And now can we change the subject?'

So it was that the following morning Slonský barged through the lobby doors, marched up to the desk and told Sergeant Mucha, 'You're the least useless desk sergeant we've had in my time here,' before climbing the stairs and getting on with his work.

Meanwhile, Krob was painstakingly working his way through reams of paper. For some reason unknown to him or, indeed, most of mankind, the fact that Vitek's bank records were kept on a computer and Krob was sitting behind a computer did not mean that the records could be sent magically from one to the other. Instead, some lucky peon at the bank had printed them all out and a courier had cycled across town to give them to Krob so that he could think about typing them all in again. Being of a methodical turn of mind, he decided that the first thing to do was to check whether there was anything useful in the bundle, to which end he was sitting with a red pencil and a blue ballpoint pen, looking for any matches between the names of people paying into or being paid from Vitek's bank account, and the list of names he had put together from the readable files in Vitek's safe. Any enthusiasm he felt for this task was tempered by the knowledge that if Spehar's wizards managed to decipher anything amidst the purple stains, a second list of names might force him to do this all over again.

'No luck yet?' said Peiperová, who had just walked in through the door.

'No matches so far. I've got about a third of the list to go.'

'I suppose if the material in the files is old, the blackmail payments may be a long time ago,' Peiperová suggested.

'That crossed my mind, but we don't have easy access to anything more than seven years old. And is it likely that a blackmailer just stopped being a blackmailer one morning?'

'I suppose not. Unless whatever secret he had wasn't a secret any longer.'

'Take a look at the list of names and see if you spot any that have been in the news about some scandal or other.'

Peiperová picked it up and began reading. 'That one's familiar — Renáta Orenková — but I can't think why. Let me do a little digging on her.'

It took only a few minutes to find out why Peiperová knew the name, so she was soon back in Krob's doorway.

'She owned a high-end women's fashion store.'

'Is she still alive?' asked Krob.

'I don't know. I didn't find an obituary for her, so perhaps she is. I'll see if I can get hold of an address for her. You keep on with the others. It might be an idea if Jerneková or I come with you when you question her.'

'You're on. After all, I don't know what I ought to be asking her about.'

Navrátil was equally frustrated in his attempts to find out what Vitek had been doing for the last twenty years. The idea had occurred to him that if he could discover whom Vitek was hanging around with, he might find a motive for the murder, on the grounds that people are more likely to be killed by people they know, but it was proving more difficult than he expected.

'It's as if he didn't want anyone to know what was going on in his life,' he commented to Slonský.

'That could be a sign of a guilty conscience,' Slonský told him. 'On the other hand, it may just be that he didn't want nosey folk like you knowing his business.'

'But he can't have stayed in his flat all that time.'

'Oh, I don't know. Not having to meet anyone could be quite appealing. Of course, I'd have to go out from time to time to get beer and sausages.'

'Exactly. You can't avoid some interactions. He's got a bank account and some investments. He still owned a couple of properties that he rented out.'

'Apartments?' Slonský asked.

'No, what used to be clubs. Maybe they still are.'

'Let's find out who rents them. Killing your landlord is one method of getting a rent reduction.'

'The leases are in the name of holding companies.'

'Ah! That's good.'

'Is it?'

'Certainly. It means we can get Major Klinger to do the donkeywork for us. Gather up the details and we'll nip upstairs and pay him a visit.'

Major Klinger, who was both head of the Fraud Squad and fifty per cent of its personnel, occupied a spartan room on the floor above. His team had once been more numerous but when one of their number had been caught turning a blind eye to infractions in exchange for little perks like holidays in Mauritius and an account at a casino in Karlovy Vary, Klinger had not been permitted to replace him lthoughugh, as Slonský pointed out at the time, if every department with a corrupt policeman was not allowed to recruit a replacement there would be a lot of empty offices in the executive corridor.

The office was spartan not because Klinger was being punished, but because he had serious concerns about germs. Over the years this had progressed from swabbing door handles before using them to having his office carpet replaced with a wipe-clean laminate once he had learned that carpets were a major threat to health. Over a glass of chilled Chablis he would recite a list of nasty organisms that liked nothing better than to snuggle into an office carpet and raise multiple families there.

Somehow Klinger had mastered the art of the clean desktop, which Slonský grudgingly admired. The latter had a stack of three trays on one corner of his desk which were his out, in and pending trays, though he was not too sure which was which, and papers accumulated in whichever one looked emptiest until Peiperová could stand it no longer and offered to file them for him, an exercise which frequently liberated unpaid expenses claims (sometimes her own) and, on one occasion, the case notes for a prosecution which Slonský had sworn blind he had returned.

Slonský knocked on the door.

'How can I help you?' Klinger asked, forcing his face into an insincere and frankly creepy smile.

'We're investigating the murder of Dominik Vitek,' Slonský replied, easing himself into a chair without waiting for an invitation. Navrátil remained standing.

'Vitek? Is he dead?'

'Oh, yes. It's one of the first things we check during a murder inquiry. It would be so embarrassing if we went to court and the victim jumped up and said he was all right now.'

'I meant that the news had not reached me.'

'Navrátil, make sure that the major gets to hear about all the cases we're investigating.'

'No need,' said Klinger. 'Just explain why you're telling me this.'

'You know who Vitek was, right?'

'Yes.'

'His bank accounts don't reveal anything suspicious to our untrained eyes. But you, with your eagle optics and superior financial knowledge, might well spot something. I'm particularly keen to know about the commercial properties he leased out. Navrátil here has discovered they're leased to holding companies, but we'd like to know who is behind those.'

Klinger had a high regard for Navrátil and had attempted to poach him on more than one occasion. 'I doubt I shall find anything that Lieutenant Navrátil hasn't, but of course I shall do my best.'

'And your best is a very good best,' announced Slonský encouragingly.

Klinger eyed him suspiciously. 'Have you been on a training course?' he asked.

'Why do you ask?'

'Unsolicited encomiums on a colleague's work are not your style.'

Slonský stood and headed for the door. 'Criminals come and criminals go,' he announced, 'but training courses go on forever.' He paused while turning the door handle, an act that he knew would irritate Klinger, who would have to give it another deep clean now. 'By the way, have you heard that Sergeant Mucha is thinking of retiring?'

Give Klinger his due, his reaction was immediate and utterly genuine. 'Mucha? Retire? No, he can't.'

'I'm glad you feel that way. A number of his friends are attempting to think of a way to dissuade him — for his own good, you understand. If you could bend your mighty brain in that direction it would be appreciated.'

'I certainly will,' Klinger responded, so perturbed by this news that he accepted the file Navrátil offered without using a handkerchief to grab it.

The next to be recruited was Colonel Rajka. He appeared in Slonský's office doorway. This was, in itself, indicative of the seriousness of the situation, since the normal course of events was for Rajka to ring Slonský and ask him to come to his office, a procedure frequently frustrated by Slonský's inability to remember which button you had to press on the phone set to pick up a call. As a result the standard procedure had been modified so that Rajka called Navrátil or Peiperová to ask them to pop next door and summon Slonský for him. But on this occasion Rajka had walked upstairs and along the corridor and was now filling the doorway, as befitted a former wrestler. As always, his uniform shirt looked immaculate and his tie was perfectly knotted. Slonský, on the other hand, had once been moved on by a city policeman when he was sheltering from the rain in a shop doorway on Old Town Square and told 'You can't sleep here — find a hostel'.

'I've heard a disquieting rumour that Mucha is thinking of retiring,' Rajka barked.

I wonder who started that, Slonský thought, seeing as most of the rumours in police headquarters were started by Mucha. Was somebody making a play to be his replacement?

'So I've heard, sir.'

'We must stop him, Slonský.'

'Agreed, sir. But how?'

'You're his oldest friend. Don't you have any ideas?'

'Apart from kidnapping him and locking him in the cells, I can't think of anything. And that won't work because then we couldn't expect him to help with all the stuff he does for us.'

'Exactly, Slonský. All the stuff he does for us. It'll be a catastrophe.'

'He's more use to the police service than that new computer system we're getting. Can't we cancel that and just give Mucha the twenty million crowns to stay?'

'Tempting, but not something I can influence, Slonský.'

'Maybe if we organise a whip-round for him as if he was leaving, but only give it to him if he doesn't…'

'What would Mucha do with the money? He seems to live quite frugally.'

'Hire a hitman to take out his sister-in-law.'

'Be serious, Slonský!'

'Then I don't know what to suggest, sir.'

'That makes two of us. But make no mistake about it, Slonský; this could be the end of civilisation as we know it.'

CHAPTER 6

'The building doesn't exactly scream "Happy Sunset", does it?' asked Peiperová, looking up at the nameboard of the nursing home.

Jerneková did not reply.

Peiperová sighed. 'Okay, you can drive on the way back.'

'Promise?'

'Promise. Now can we resume talking to each other?'

'Never stopped. I just didn't have anything to say.'

'That's not like you.'

'I was concentrating on mentally changing gear and working the pedals.'

Peiperová pulled into a parking space and the two detectives clambered out.

'You can't park there!'

The owner of the voice was a large woman in a lavender fleece jogging suit.

'Why not?' asked Peiperová.

'The doctor parks there when he comes.'

'Are you expecting him?'

'No. But he might turn up. And then he'll have nowhere to park.'

Peiperová produced her police ID. 'I'll move it if we need to. I rang earlier. We've come to talk to Ms Orenková.'

The woman eyed them suspiciously. 'Nobody told me. What's it about?'

'It's in connection with a murder enquiry.'

'She can't have done it. She's barely mobile these days.'

'We don't suspect her of involvement in it. She may have known the victim.'

'Oh, God, that's all we need. Try not to upset her, or we'll have histrionics for days. Highly strung, you know.'

'It'll be the artistic side in her,' Peiperová replied.

'Glad I haven't got one, then,' Jerneková muttered.

The lavender bundle waddled up the steps and announced, 'Room 12! She'll be getting a coffee in a few minutes. Do you two want one?'

'Can we have two?' Jerneková said. 'One each, you see.'

The woman nodded and pinballed her way along the narrow corridor. 'It'll be open,' she called over her shoulder. 'She won't be going anywhere.'

The detectives found the door and knocked. There was no reply, so they knocked again.

'Probably deaf,' said Jerneková. 'Shall we just go in?'

Peiperová turned the handle and knocked again as she opened the door. There was nobody there. 'Ms Orenková?' she called.

'Behind the screen, dear,' came a cultivated voice. 'Be out in a jiffy. Just having a piddle.'

A few seconds later the screen was pushed back and a tiny woman emerged. She looked as if she was about to go out for cocktails. She wore a white dress with enormous red poppies on it and a set of pearls large enough to make her look as if she had a toilet seat round her neck. The outfit was completed with bright red patent leather shoes. Jerneková was relieved to see that they only had five-centimetre heels, so she still experienced the relatively unusual feeling of being taller than another adult.

'I'm so sorry,' Renáta Orenková began. 'Not being in a position to greet my guests. Do sit down if you can find somewhere. I'm afraid I shall have to have the recliner chair or I'll never get myself back up again.'

When she was settled, complete with two cushions at her back and her feet on a small stool because her bunions were giving her some trouble (but of course one isn't properly dressed without good shoes) they were able to begin.

'They didn't tell me why you wanted to talk to me,' she said. 'Not that it matters. It's lovely to have visitors whatever the reason.'

'I'm afraid we may have some bad news for you,' Peiperová said. 'Do you know a man called Dominik Vitek?'

'Dominik…? Dominik … Vitek … ah! Yes, dear, dear Dominik. How is he? I haven't seen him for years.'

'I'm sorry to have to tell you that he is dead,' Peiperová replied solemnly.

'Yes, somebody battered … ow! That was my ankle!' Jerneková added.

'So sorry!' Peiperová continued, turning to her colleague to give her an angry glare. 'Clumsy of me.'

'Somebody battered…?' Renáta repeated.

'Somebody battered on the door and found him dead when he didn't reply,' Peiperová responded.

'Oh! How very sad. In his flat, was he? Had he been there long?'

'We'll have to wait for the pathologist to tell us that.'

'No, dear, I meant had he lived there long? Dominik used to have a divine little villa near the Central Park, you know, out near Lužiny. But when he retired he said he'd move a bit nearer town so it wasn't such a chore to get to the theatre.' The old woman chuckled. 'Although I suspect he was more worried about getting home again after the show! Taxis aren't cheap and it would have been very unwise of Dominik to drive, I fear.'

'He liked a drop of wine, did he?' Jerneková interjected.

'More than a drop, dear. When he was with his theatrical friends he could be himself, you see. He was such fun! And very kind to me.'

'That may be what we wanted to ask you about,' Peiperová said. 'We found your name in one of his files, and we wondered why he had made a note. There was also a photograph.'

'Really? May I see it?'

Peiperová removed it from her bag and held it in front of Renáta without letting go of it.

'Now, where are my glasses?'

'On a string around your neck,' Jerneková bellowed, it being her firm belief that all old people are hard of hearing.

'Ah, thank you. Let me see. My word! I wonder why Dominik kept this.'

Tact was required now, which was why Peiperová motioned to her colleague to keep her mouth shut. 'You seem to be on very good terms with the man in this photograph.'

'I was, then.'

'Then?'

'I don't remember exactly when this was taken but that dress — a divine little thing in crêpe de Chine with such a pretty plaited belt in mint green leather — I could never forget. Do you see those tiny diamanté tips on the collar edge? So clever and delicate. And so feminine. In those days women weren't afraid to look feminine. When one danced, the skirt would balloon ever so slightly without being in any way immodest.'

Peiperová interrupted the fashion history lesson to bring her back to the subject in hand. 'The man?' she prompted.

'Oh, yes. Well, that's Viktor.'

'Viktor?'

'My husband.'

'Can you think of any reason why Dominik Vitek would have kept a picture of your husband?'

'Not at all. He didn't like him.'

'No?'

'Good heavens, no. In fact, that's what I meant when I said that dear Dominik was so kind to me.'

A carer knocked and delivered a tray of coffee.

'Oh, how lovely! The best china too. I am being spoiled,' Renáta announced gleefully. 'Will you pour, please? My hand won't hold that heavy coffee-pot these days.'

Jerneková could not argue with that. Renáta's wrists looked no bigger than a small child's. She laid out the cups and poured the dark coffee into them.

'This is so like the old days! Do you know, I can almost imagine we're all going out together for supper and a lovely natter.'

'Where would women have been able to go in those days?' Jerneková artlessly inquired.

'Ah, well, there we must thank Dominik again. There was an old building in a street behind Wenceslas Square and he converted it into a very smart parlour called The Ladies' Lounge. We all used to meet up there. And there were a pair of hulking men at the foot of the stairs who saw to it that we weren't bothered. Men weren't as respectful of women then as they are now.'

Jerneková opened her mouth to argue but saw Peiperová's warning glance just in time.

'We girls could have a glass of wine and a good gossip free from men.'

'That must have been fun,' Peiperová commented, encouraging her to keep talking.

'Oh, it was! And then Dominik would put us into taxis to go home. Ah, happy days!'

'You were explaining how Dominik had been kind to you.'

'Was I? I'm so sorry, I was far away for a moment. Well, this photograph must have been taken about forty years ago. My husband was very involved in politics — it never appealed to me — and he got permission for me to open a little dress shop. We were so happy. And because my husband worked for the trade ministry, he had plenty of overseas trips, and I would go with him and make contacts. I imported some very exclusive lines, you see.'

'How could you pay for them? Surely foreign suppliers wouldn't want Czech crowns?' Peiperová asked.

'My husband used to arrange it for me. Sometimes he'd get hold of Western currency. But usually we'd pay in furs. The Russians paid the government for things with furs, if they paid at all, and we'd use the furs to buy the things I wanted. I remember we once sold a couple of trucks to buy some charming French lingerie.' She clapped her hands in delight at the memory.

'And then?'

'Ah. Well, Dominik was involved with some dissidents, and Viktor told me the Party weren't happy about it, and I had to leave The Ladies' Lounge. I was so upset. I told Dominik and he was very good about it, and said that he would have a word with Viktor to see if he couldn't change his mind.'

'And did he?'

'Did he what, dear?'

'Did he change his mind?'

'Not exactly. Suddenly there was an awful fuss because the security people had somehow got hold of some papers that suggested that Viktor had sold off some rifles and pocketed the money. Dominik came to see me and said that for my own safety I ought to divorce Viktor otherwise I would go down with him, so I did.'

'And what happened to Viktor?'

'I don't really know. He lost his job and I heard he'd gone to prison for quite a long time, but I've never seen him again. Anyway, Dominik was somehow able to get me the money I needed to keep going. I gave it up in the end, of course. Tastes change and young women today would rather have a lot of cheap tat than a few quality pieces.' Suspecting that she may have offended them she quickly added, 'But I'm talking about things for special occasions, not work clothes. I imagine the police make you wear very … practical things.'

The detectives smiled weakly and sipped their coffee.

Slonský listened to the women's report with interest. 'So this Viktor — what was it again?'

'Skála. Viktor Skála,' Peiperová supplied.

'Viktor Skála was fingered for misappropriation of state property and went down. How long for?'

'I don't know, sir. The records on the computer don't go back that far.'

'Just as well we have an alternative source of mid-Seventies information, then. Come on!' He led them downstairs to the front desk where Mucha was laboriously entering names in a large book. He glanced up at the new arrivals before returning to his task.

'Don't bother. I'm not changing my mind,' he said.

'We weren't going to ask about that,' Slonský replied, 'though since you've mentioned it, when do you have to put your notice in?'

'About three weeks. But if it wasn't that, what are you after? I know that look. It's your "I'm about to ask for the world but I'm being sly about it" look.'

'I'm hurt! When have I ever been less than straightforward with you?'

'Do you want a complete catalogue or just the last two hundred instances?'

Slonský turned to his assistants. 'Peiperová, when you come round to collect for Mucha's leaving present, remind me to put a hundred crowns less in than I was going to do.'

'*You're* going to put more than a hundred crowns in a leaving kitty?' Jerneková blurted out before rubbing her leg and continuing, 'I'm going to start wearing shinpads to work.'

Slonský bent his neck slightly to speak quietly into Peiperová's ear. 'It's not regarded as good management to kick assistants, however satisfying it may be at the time. It can land you in hot water. Take it from one who knows.' He leaned on the counter. 'If you're not busy…' he began.

'I am,' Mucha replied.

'Well, when you're not busy…'

'I won't be. I'm always busy.'

'Maybe one of us can give you a hand with that.'

'You can't. I wish you could, but you can't. I've got to enter the names of lawyers who visit clients in the cells. When did lawyers' firms' names get so damn long?' He held up a business card for inspection.

'Why don't you just stick the card in the book?' Jerneková suggested.

'Because I have to keep a record of who comes and goes and when.'

'So write the times next to the cards,' she said.

Mucha thought for a moment, then slammed the book shut. 'I'll do it later,' he said.

'Now, since you appear to be momentarily unoccupied,' Slonský smoothly commenced, 'you can do us a great service.'

'How much?' asked Mucha resignedly. 'I've only got two hundred crowns on me.'

'I'm not after a loan.'

'You're not?'

'No.'

'Sorry. I just thought that's the spiel you usually give me before you ask for the price of a lunch.'

'You have a low opinion of me,' Slonský said reprovingly.

'No, I have a better opinion of you than most people.'

'Be that as it may, I need your considerable talents. Viktor Skála.'

'I'm not Viktor Skála.'

'I know you're not.'

'Then why did you call me Viktor Skála?'

'I didn't.'

'I just heard you.'

'I hadn't finished the sentence. Viktor Skála was apparently sent to jail on the word of an informer about thirty years ago. I would love to know who the informer was, just in case it was our murder victim and Viktor Skála is now out of jail and did it.'

Mucha sucked his teeth. 'Thirty years ago, you say?'

'Give or take.'

'That's in the communist years.'

'Ten out of ten for your historical knowledge. But can you find the file?'

'What kind of crime was it? If it was political, forget it. Not a lot was committed to paper and they were the first files burned when the StB realised how the wind was blowing.'

'Allegedly,' Slonský told him, 'he was done for flogging off state property and pocketing the proceeds.'

'In that event,' Mucha replied, stroking his chin in thought, 'the regime probably cranked up the publicity and there may be some newspaper cuttings to give us a fix on the date. Any chance of getting hold of those?'

'I could ask Valentin.'

'Was his paper being published then?'

'No, but he knows where some of the archives from the old papers went.'

'You get him on to that and I'll see what I can dig up. But it's a long shot.'

'If anyone can find it, you can,' Slonský said, giving his old friend an affectionate squeeze on the shoulder.

'I'm still not changing my mind,' Mucha replied, and said it twice more as they walked away from him.

CHAPTER 7

'Skála. Skála,' murmured Valentin.

'Viktor Skála,' Slonský elaborated.

'Doesn't immediately ring a bell.'

'Well, it was a long shot. You must have attended dozens of trials as a young reporter.'

'Excuse me, but by the mid-Seventies I was a senior correspondent. And trials of corrupt officials weren't that common. Not public ones anyway. A lot of the time they were just put on a train to Slovakia and told not to come back. Only the really serious ones went to trial.'

'This one did. His wife was told he went to jail for quite a while.'

'I wonder who told her? If I was her I'd have gone into hiding as fast as possible and made it hard for anyone to tell me anything.'

Slonský drained his second glass of the evening. 'That's a good point,' he said. 'I'd have done the same. Anyway, is there any chance that you can find anything about the case?'

'Funny,' said Valentin, 'I just mentioned Slovakia.'

'What's that got to do with it?'

'Fill my glass again and I'll tell you. It's looking lonely though. It would like a little pear brandy to keep it company.'

Slonský attracted a waiter with some gentle abuse and arranged their order. Once it was delivered Valentin picked up his story again.

'I didn't know this at the time, but it seems that just before the Wall came down the authorities realised what was going to happen and destroyed a lot of files. And if they couldn't destroy the files they wrecked the indexes to make the files harder to search.'

'Of course you knew it. We all did.'

'Let me finish. The bit I didn't know then was that while this was very efficiently done in Prague, the further you got from the big city the less effort was put into it. And by the time you got to eastern Slovakia they didn't try that hard at all. They prioritised the cases of local interest — the ones that were likely to get their perpetrators hanging from lamp-posts when the wind shifted.'

'And?'

'So it's quite possible that if anything still exists it may be in the archives out there. I've got a couple of contacts. I'll give them a ring. They owe me a favour.'

'How?'

'How what?'

'How do they come to owe you a favour?'

Valentin airily waved the question away. 'Oh, I send them stories from Prague. Saves them a trip. They pocket the expenses and go fishing for a day or two and I write a story for them.'

'What's in it for you?'

'Reciprocity. Any big stories that break in Slovakia they'll cover for me. After all, who the hell wants to go to Slovakia? I mean, Bratislava's okay, but there's a large part of the country that still hasn't heard of indoor plumbing and floorboards.'

Slonský did not share the stereotypical Czech prejudice against Slovaks. In his view, Slovaks were human beings (despite appearances) with feelings and needs, and often very easy to collar because the criminal classes were thicker than their Czech counterparts. He remembered with affection a jewel thief who had come to Prague and had a very successful weekend and was just on the tram to the railway station to go back home with tens of thousands of crowns'-worth of jewellery in his knapsack when he thought he'd save some cash by not buying a ticket and was duly challenged by a transport inspector. Mistaking him for a plain-clothes policeman, he took a swing at him and was wrestled to the ground. On completing the arrest Slonský inspected the rucksack, as much in hope of a sandwich he could confiscate as in expectation of any evidence there, and was pleasantly surprised to find that he had solved several recent crimes in one fell swoop.

'You find out what you can, old friend. Anything will be welcome.'

Valentin sipped his pear brandy and sighed with satisfaction. 'That other matter,' he said. 'I may have an idea.'

'Other matter?'

'The great story of the present day.'

'You've had an idea about keeping Mucha? I'm all ears.'

'It's a variation on an idea of yours, really. Remember when you were trying to ensure that Colonel Urban got the job as Director of Police?'

'Of course I do.'

'You suggested to him that it would do his candidacy no harm if he got himself shot in the line of duty.'

'You want me to get Mucha shot? There's a lot less flesh on Mucha than there was on Urban. With the colonel a shot in the thigh would have been quite safe. There's hardly any part of Mucha that doesn't have an important organ underneath.'

'That's not quite…'

'Besides which, I knew a few decent shots who had nothing against Urban. I don't know who I'd ask who could be trusted not to settle old scores with Mucha for booking him in.'

'I wasn't thinking of shooting him. I was thinking of getting him a gallantry award.'

'Gallantry? Mucha?'

'It's not that hard to grasp, Josef.'

'You didn't see how fast he ducked when the lights in the station lobby short-circuited. He's a lovely man but he's not gallantry medal material.'

'Nobody ever is. Read the comments of their friends. They nearly always say they didn't know he had it in him.'

'That's true.'

'And it doesn't have to be true. You just have to concoct a story that makes him sound like a hero.'

'But he'll know he isn't.'

'Not if he gets knocked out early on. We just need to stage something threatening, cause a lot of confusion so nobody really knows what's happening, knock Mucha out and tell him afterwards how brave he was and put him up for a medal.'

Slonský took a large gulp of beer and rolled it round his mouth while he thought. 'That is, without doubt, the daftest idea I've heard for a long time. But since we don't have any other ideas, let's run with it. But we really need an unimpeachable witness to back me up about Mucha's bravery. And he's got to be gullible enough to be taken in by whatever story we spin him about the confusion.'

They thought for a moment before chorusing, 'Major Lukas!'

Mucha was a systematic researcher. Many a postgraduate student at the Charles University could have learned from his methods. He had found a starting point, because he already knew about The Ladies' Lounge. As a young policeman he had been sent there one evening to sort out an altercation between Dominik Vitek's security guards and some goons sent by the local Communist Party branch to cause trouble there. As it happened, he could also remember the date, because it was his wife's twenty-sixth birthday, and therefore it must have been in 1977. It was likely that if Skála had warned his wife off going there, this was around that time. Since Skála was not senior enough to have known in advance what was being planned, Mucha at least had a date to work from.

He then reasoned that this would not have been the only harassment directed at Vitek, so he needed to see any contemporary files about Vitek. He called up Vitek's current file, from which he gleaned that Vitek had been an exemplary citizen for many years, but there was an older paper file for which he now had an index number and a location. Thus armed he put on his uniform jacket, told Officer Fintr he was going out, took a tram and a bus, and in around forty minutes he was thumping on the side door of a building adjoining a railway goods yard.

The young policeman at the desk was as helpful as anyone could be when they do not know what they are doing, and allowed himself to be bamboozled by Mucha's detailed knowledge of the file he wanted and the long-established rule in the Czech Republic that if you know a file exists, you are probably entitled to see it. A few minutes later Mucha was helping the young man search through the stacks for a crate.

'You know, this would be a lot easier if the crates were in numerical order,' Mucha suggested.

'I know, but where do you begin? I don't even know what the first number here is.'

After a quarter of an hour or so they found a small village of boxes from the mid-Seventies, and a few minutes after that Mucha had the crate open in front of him and was rummaging through it for Vitek's file, while keeping an eye open for anything about Skála at the same time.

'Is there somewhere I can spread this out?' he finally asked, holding up a file labelled *Vitek, Dominik*.

'There's a reading desk in the back room. I'm supposed to watch you to make sure the papers are safe, though, and I can't leave the front desk.'

'Then how would it be,' Mucha went on in his best speaking-to-a-small-child voice, 'if I used a corner of your countertop to read this?'

The young man beamed. 'That would be fine.'

'Then that's what I'll do.'

Mucha had no sooner opened the folder than the officer declared that he was off to make coffee for them both and left Mucha completely unattended.

When reading these old files a certain amount of interpretation between the lines was necessary. For example, Vitek had been fined for littering the street. This was probably because the city refuse team had stopped collecting from his premises so that they would have an excuse to fine him.

There was the depressingly common litany of small offences catalogued to justify the state's harassment, but the real meat came in the section headed "Known associations". The names were predominantly female. Renáta was there under her married name of Skálová with a red line connecting her to Viktor Skála. Gratifyingly, someone had pencilled a reference number next to Skála's name, probably a link to a personal folder devoted to him which Mucha could look for in a minute. He had taken up two pages of his notebook with the names of contacts when he was brought up short by the next name on the list. He knew her.

Věra Slonská.

*

Technician First Class Spehar had worked wonders on the stained papers. Slonský marvelled as he turned them over and over in his hands. 'You can barely see the purple dye at all,' he admitted.

'That's because it's not the same paper. We took images of the pages using a range of filters and then reprinted them on fresh sheets. We've lost odd bits here and there. In some cases there was enough to let us make an educated guess at the words — we've underlined those on the copies. A couple of patches right next to the explosion weren't recoverable so we've put black shapes to show those sections.'

Slonský leafed through them when Spehar had gone. So far as he could see, the only thing that was any different to the files he had already looked at was that these were newer. Navrátil returned from some errand or other and was invited to look at them too. 'Anything come to mind, lad?'

'I don't see anything here worth killing for.'

'No. But somebody did.'

'Or maybe they thought there was something that doesn't actually exist. Remember that gym killings case you told me about?'

'What gym killings?' chimed in Krob as he entered the room.

'Some lads told a man that there was a hole in the wall through which they'd all been watching his wife in the women's showers,' explained Slonský. 'He killed two and wounded four more, and it turned out there was no such hole, and they'd just concocted a tale to wind him up because they knew he got jealous.'

'It worked then,' Krob said.

'Yes, it did. He even stabbed an old man who just happened to be changing in the corner where they said the hole was. He was lucky. He died. Life after someone rams a hunting knife into your temple wouldn't have been good.'

They sat in silence for a moment.

'I don't suppose whoever it was actually found what they wanted,' Krob suggested.

'There was no sign of the safe being opened,' Navrátil answered.

'But the killer could have calmly shut it before they left,' Krob pointed out. 'You need the combination to open a safe, but anyone can shut it.'

'So whatever it was had already been taken out?' Slonský asked. 'Presumably by Vitek. But why?'

'He'd reached a deal with whomever he was blackmailing,' Krob suggested.

Slonský shook his head. 'If Vitek was a blackmailer — and we have no evidence of that at the moment — he'd been at it a long time. He wasn't stupid enough to sit with the material in his flat while the killer counts out banknotes before topping him and taking the folder and his money. Vitek had the whip hand. He'd have taken the money and maybe handed over copies, promising that the real thing would come by post, or be left in a locker somewhere a hundred kilometres away.' Slonský lobbed the papers into Krob's lap. 'Add these to your list and see if any of the names mean anything to anyone. Trace anyone you can pin down. Something wrong, Navrátil?'

'I thought this was my case.'

'Oh, yes. I forgot.'

Mucha knew he could not keep it a secret from Slonský, but he was trying to think of a way of giving him the information without causing a wicked rise in blood pressure. Maybe, he thought, this was an occasion when he needed a bit of lateral thinking. Perhaps his best bet was to get to the bottom of the matter before he told Slonský that Věra was involved. If he could show that it was a mistake or the result of some misapprehension on the part of the security services, his old friend's mind would be put at ease.

He locked the other material that he had found in a drawer. He was unsure whether, if he took it to Slonský now, something about his demeanour would start the detective asking awkward questions and Slonský would wheedle it out of him; which, of course, would be worse because he had not immediately volunteered it, which would make Slonský think that Mucha was only telling part of the story that he had unearthed and that there was something awful in the files that he, Slonský, could not get at without Mucha's help. And Slonský would stop trusting Mucha, which would bring the number of people that Slonský trusted in the world down to a total of … minus one.

He logged in to the residency database to see if he could find Věra's address. She was the only Slonská on the screen, so he copied down the details from her most recent national identity card application. Officer Fintr was a good lad. He could be left on his own a little while longer, Mucha thought, but given the awkward journey across town to Věra's apartment he asked by radio if any police cars were free to give him a lift part of the way. One diverted to headquarters to pick him up and dropped him on the main road about two hundred metres from her home.

Mucha knew Věra of old. He had met her when she married Slonský and although they had not been very close then, it had pained him when she had walked out on his friend after only two years of marriage to live with a poet. The poet turned out to be as unreliable as mothers believe that poets are, and the relationship had come to grief within a couple of months, though nobody had known that until about two and a half years ago, when she reappeared to tell Slonský she had never signed the divorce papers and they were therefore still legally married. Not without some misgivings, Slonský had allowed himself to be talked into going out with her to see if the relationship could be rekindled, and all seemed to be going well until her birthday when a drunk came up to Slonský and warned him against the woman across the table who had left him after living together for three years that she had somehow forgotten to mention to Slonský.

He found the building, a rather rundown block of three storeys with chunks of render missing from the front and a concerning crack above a door lintel. There was no lift, so he climbed a flight of stairs and knocked on the door. There was no answer.

There was no letterbox and no glass in the front door, and Mucha was deciding what to do next when a woman appeared at the door across the hall.

'I thought it wouldn't be long before you lot turned up. You're too late. She's done a runner.'

'You know Věra?'

'Oh, yes, we all know Věra. Good riddance to bad rubbish is what I say. Too stuck-up for the likes of us, wasn't she, but then she comes home one day and next thing she's dragging her suitcase to a taxi and she's off.'

'When was this?' asked Mucha.

'I don't know exactly. About two weeks ago, maybe.'

Or, to put it another way, thought Mucha, just after Dominik Vitek was killed.

CHAPTER 8

Dr Novák dropped his folder on Slonský's desk with the air of a man who never wanted to see it again. 'Nothing we didn't already know about the cause of death,' he said. 'A hefty whack to the right side of the head with a large heavy object. Bone fragments did a lot of damage and he bled profusely inside his skull. No sign of anything untoward in the toxicology report. Last meal was about four hours before death. Tripe.'

'Tripe?'

'Tripe.'

'I didn't think anyone still ate tripe. Hang on — I don't remember seeing any signs that anyone had been cooking tripe there. Anything in the waste bin?'

'I thought of that,' Novák replied smugly. 'He must have eaten out.'

'I wonder if he was on his own.'

'You think he met his murderer for lunch? Unlikely, I'd have thought. The killer couldn't make polite conversation for four hours before clubbing Vitek to death.'

'Maybe they were negotiating.'

'No coffee cups, no drinks glasses. My bet would be that he'd just let the killer in when he was attacked.'

'We're presuming the killer was a man. Could it have been a woman?'

'It could have been a kangaroo for all I know. No prints, and the pan had been given a quick if ineffective wipe. Anyone strong enough to lift a frying pan could have done it. And a lot of women lift frying pans on a regular basis, I believe.'

Slonský lobbed the report in the general direction of his in-tray (or possibly his out-tray) and leaned back in his chair for a good stretch. 'You don't have tripe for breakfast,' he announced, 'so let's assume it was lunch. And he was killed four hours later. And we were called around four o'clock. Coincidence?'

'You were called around four o'clock at least a week later.'

Novák turned for the door. 'I'm a pathologist, not a psychologist. But whoever it was didn't bring a weapon with them, so it doesn't sound like a premeditated killing. Maybe something got out of hand and they regretted it afterwards and wanted to make sure he was found.'

'Or maybe they live in the building and couldn't stand the smell of decomposing neighbour.'

Mucha had been agonising over his next step when a blinding light of revelation came over him. He did not have to think what he was going to say to Slonský because he had just remembered that Slonský had said it was Navrátil's case. He would lay the facts in front of Navrátil and let the young lieutenant decide what was to be done. It was what he was paid for, after all.

The difficulty lay in trying to speak to Navrátil without Slonský's knowledge, given that they often shared an office. No opportunity had presented itself for a couple of days, but then Mucha spotted Slonský chatting to Novák in the canteen and realised that Navrátil was not there. That meant he was in exactly the right place, namely, somewhere else, so Mucha ran back to the front desk and rang Navrátil on his mobile phone. 'Can we talk?' Mucha asked.

'We're talking now,' Navrátil responded.

'I mean face to face, without Slonský.'

'Without Captain Slonský?'

The tone of Navrátil's voice betrayed his concern that Mucha might be about to suggest something improper, like withholding information from a superior.

'A situation has developed which needs delicate handling,' Mucha whispered, 'and it concerns the captain.'

'I see,' said Navrátil, though actually he did not.

'It's in connection with the case you're working on.'

'So your trip to the archive wasn't a complete washout?'

'Far from it. But I haven't reported back because I don't know how best to do it.'

Navrátil grasped the problem, at least in outline. 'It'll have to be somewhere Captain Slonský can be guaranteed not to go. I'll see you in the police gym in twenty minutes.'

'I've stalled as long as I can,' Mucha explained. 'I've told him that the archive custodian is looking for Skála's file for me — which is true, by the way — but if it's there he'll find it soon and I'll need to produce my list.'

'We can't suppress it,' Navrátil replied. 'It's a murder enquiry, after all. But what's causing you all this grief?'

Mucha looked about him for eavesdroppers, then produced a folder from beneath his greatcoat.

'I wondered why you were wearing that in this weather,' Navrátil said.

'I'm sweating like three-day-old pork,' Mucha answered, 'but I had to get the file out without being seen. Fifth page, look down the names of known associates of Dominik Vitek.'

Navrátil did as he was asked. 'Oh, heavens!' he exclaimed.

'Exactly.'

'I'd best interview her. Have you got her address?'

'I looked up the residency database and went there, but she's just moved out.'

'By "just" you mean…?'

'Around the time Vitek was killed.'

'Oh, heavens!'

'I hope I've done the right thing by bringing it to you,' Mucha mumbled.

'Yes, yes, of course you have,' Navrátil replied, hoping that his quavering voice was not betraying his strong wish that Mucha had not done so. 'Well, the fact remains that we need to interview her, and to do that we need to find her. Any ideas?'

'We could ask the tax people for information about her employer and see if we can contact her through them. But if she's run out on them too it won't be looking good for her.'

'No,' agreed Navrátil, 'it certainly won't.'

If Jerneková had been a little older she would have recognised the name Lenka Lipská in a flash. For a decade everyone knew her as the indulgent mother whose son and daughter formed part of the clever gang of children who uncovered dastardly capitalist plots against the regime week by week in a popular television programme of the Sixties. Most of the adventures ended with the mother sitting her children down at the kitchen table and saying, "I'll give you each a glass of milk and you can tell me all about it."

When the series ended Lipská was so firmly typecast in Czech minds as the slightly dotty and ineffectual mother that she struggled to find work. She provided the voices for cartoon characters and puppets and for one awful summer perambulated the streets of Prague dressed as Minnie Mouse. An enterprising milk company used her (and her catchphrase) in their commercials for a while until public recognition was no longer there and the sentence lost its ready connection.

The identification was further complicated by the fact that Lenka was not her real name. Originally named Dagmar, she adopted the name Lenka after the war because she liked the alliteration and it made her sound a bit less Germanic. However, when Slonský happened to spot Vitek's file on Lipská on Jerneková's desk, he knew immediately who she was.

'Lenka Lipská, eh!'

'You know her, sir?'

'Doesn't everyone?'

'Er — no.'

'Ah, before your time. The nation's favourite mother.'

'Come again?'

'Star of a television programme. She ran the perfect family — husband who wore a tie even when he wasn't at work, two blonde-haired children who never had spots or dental work and always did their homework, Grandpa who could fix anything in a shed he had under a big oak tree. Mother always had a sparkling white apron and wore shoes with heels while she was doing the cooking, which was always restaurant-standard when she carried it to the table. She never raised her voice, always had impeccable make-up and was fiercely loyal to the Communist Party.'

'Thank goodness for that. Until that last bit I thought you were describing me.'

'They had a strangely elastic apartment as I recall. If you looked at it from the outside you couldn't work out how all the rooms fitted inside — unless Grandpa slept in the shed, I suppose. Anyway, you aren't looking at her file to join her fan club. What does it say?'

'She was a member of The Ladies' Lounge. But even after it closed she kept in touch. There are letters in there from the last ten years asking Vitek for help.'

'What kind of help?'

'She keeps going on about how she was finding it hard to get work and what she did find didn't pay well and she had to pay for accommodation on theatre runs in the provinces. She asked hm if he could use his contacts to find her work in Prague. And he must have sent her money because she thanks him from time to time for helping her to keep the wolf from the door.' Jerneková picked a letter from the pile and read a section. 'She says, "I'm not a vain woman, but you have to maintain a certain appearance for the public's sake, and that costs money I don't have. I'm reduced to looking for outfits in thrift shops. Without you, dear Dominik, I don't know what I would do." And she enclosed a signed photograph — "To Dominik, my greatest support, with love, Lenka." There you are, sir.'

'No address on the letter, though. He obviously knew it. See if you can find it among that lot.'

'I've tried. I can't. In fact, there are a couple of letters where the address has been cut off. There is one lead — she wrote to him from a hotel in Břeclav. I thought I'd see if she gave an address when she registered, but it was four or five years ago.'

'Good start, lass. You realise this knocks one of our theories on the head, don't you?'

'Sir?'

'Well, it's an unusual blackmailer who sends money to his victims.'

Jerneková found the hotel's telephone number and rang to ask them to check their registers. Understandably they were reluctant to give out such sensitive information to an unknown person on the telephone. After all, the duty manager pointed out, anyone could say that they were from the police.

Her next step was to call the local police station in Břeclav, who agreed to send a uniformed officer to the hotel to photograph the relevant page of the register, though they politely declined her other request, namely, to give the duty manager a good kick up the arse.

The tax office still had the same address for Věra Slonská that Mucha had visited, but promised to contact Navrátil if an amendment came in, though they pointed out that this was only likely if she found a new job, her last known one having ended about three months earlier.

'So what is she living on?' Navrátil pondered.

'Is she old enough to have a pension?' asked Krob.

'The captain isn't, so I doubt that she is. She must be getting some kind of benefit.'

'I'll get in touch with the Labour Office to see if she has signed on for unemployment benefit.'

'That would be good — and remember, maximum discretion. It's probably best if we don't mention this to anyone else.'

That sort of instruction always puzzled Krob, because he never talked about work at home and he had no difficulty in not talking about it to anyone else unless they needed to know something. Surely keeping silence would be harder for Navrátil, whose wife was just two offices away, separated only by the small office that Slonský tried to avoid using; the one he still referred to as "Lukas' office", although his former boss had been in the executive corridor ever since Slonský had been made a captain.

His silence was immediately tested by Jerneková, who poked her head around the door to check all was well before stepping inside.

'What are you doing?' she demanded to know.

'The same as you, I suppose,' Krob replied. 'Trying to find something in the names connected to Vitek's death.'

'Ah, good!' beamed Jerneková. 'Maybe you can help me with one of mine.' She marched towards the desk, causing Krob to hurriedly close the file he was working on and shove it in a drawer.

'Just making space,' he claimed feebly.

'We've found one more of the women, Lenka Lipská. Or at least we've got a lead. We haven't actually found her. She registered at a hotel in Břeclav and had to give her home address. The local police have just sent over a copy of the page in the registration book, but I can't read it. So I thought I'd ask a couple of fellows who have been here longer than I have.' She unrolled her photocopy of the page and pointed dramatically to the entry under "Address". 'Mean anything to you?' she asked.

Navrátil came to lend his eyes but shook his head. It took a moment or two for Krob to decipher Lenka's exuberant handwriting, but then he slowly smiled. 'The devil!' he exclaimed. 'I think it says Portheimka 45.'

'Portheimka?' said Navrátil. 'That doesn't make sense.'

'There isn't such a place as Portheimka,' said Jerneková, now thoroughly puzzled.

'There certainly is,' replied Krob, leaping from his chair to point at the large map of Prague on the wall behind him. 'But it's a park. It won't have a building number. She has given an imaginary address.'

'She probably didn't want anyone who saw her name in the book to know where she lived,' Navrátil interjected. 'Celebrities wouldn't.'

'But she'd have had to show her ID card to register,' Jerneková said. 'The address wouldn't have matched.'

'She could have said she had just moved,' Krob replied. 'Or that one was her home and the other was her agent's office which would be more useful because she was travelling so much. Or even just told them it was false and asked them not to give her secret away. The hotel would have the real address somewhere, but not in the registration book.'

'Then what's the point of the registration book?' snarled Jerneková.

'It's only really useful for foreigners,' Navrátil explained.

'How many foreigners bother to go to Břeclav?'

'I don't know. But there are at least two on that page.'

Krob had an idea. 'All may not be lost. She picked Portheimka because it sounds like it might be a street. Presumably she knows it. So perhaps she lives nearby. It might even be that if someone did write to Portheimka 45 the postwoman would know to divert it to the right address.'

Navrátil's face lit up. 'And she wouldn't pick a number at random. She'd probably pick 45 because she actually lives at number 45, but in one of the streets nearby,' he added.

'Great!' Jerneková grumbled. 'So I'm going to have to go round the houses looking for a number 45 in one of the nearby streets.'

'It's not as bad as it sounds, Lucie,' Krob assured her. 'There aren't that many streets nearby and a lot of those buildings are now offices. It's worth a try, anyway.'

'You wouldn't like to help?'

'I'd love to, but I've got too much to do here, I'm afraid.'

Jerneková looked steadily at Krob without saying anything.

'If only I was driving I could give you a lift to that part of town,' he added, rubbing his injured shoulder.

She continued to look at him.

'I suppose you could drive while I sit with you.'

'I'll get my coat,' she announced, and left before he could change his mind.

Much to Jerneková's surprise, Krob turned out to be right. They parked their car, if "parked" does justice to Jerneková's technique of aiming the nearside wheel at a kerb until she heard it crunch and then swinging the steering wheel frantically, and methodically walked the streets looking at all the buildings numbered 45. Some were offices or other non-residential buildings, but after a couple of hours they came to a tall building with an array of brass buttons by the doorway, one of which was labelled Lipská. They rang, and a querulous female voice asked what they wanted.

'Police, Ms Lipská,' said Jerneková. 'We'd like to ask you a few questions.'

'It was all a misunderstanding,' came the reply. 'I thought my friend had paid for the drinks.'

'It's not about that, Ms Lipská. You may be able to help us with a serious enquiry.'

'Serious, you say?'

'Very serious.'

'Very serious?'

'It couldn't be more serious.'

'You'd better come in. Third floor right.'

The door buzzed and they pushed it open. To their surprise the building that looked so immaculate outside had a dark hallway with no working light bulb on the ground floor and two bicycles obstructing access to the rear door.

'We'd better have a word with the building's owner,' Krob murmured. 'If there was a fire they'd never get to the back door.'

'One thing at a time,' Jerneková replied. 'At least we don't have to worry about an elevator failure during a fire, because there isn't one. We'll have to traipse up the stairs. And no pushing on my bum till I give you permission.'

'I wouldn't dream of it,' Krob answered indignantly.

'I'll probably give you permission about halfway up the second flight,' Jerneková added. 'These steps are high if you've only got little legs.'

They reached the door which remained resolutely shut. Krob knocked while Jerneková got her breath back, and presently they heard the rasping of a chain being withdrawn and the clunk of a couple of bolts before the door opened just enough for a watery blue eye to peek out at them.

Krob showed his identification and moved aside to let Jerneková do the same, at which Lipská stepped back and allowed them in.

'I'm sorry,' she said. 'You can't be too careful these days. Wretched autograph hunters.'

'If I may,' Krob said quietly, 'the chain should stay on until you're happy that your visitors are respectable. I could have pushed the door open and forced my way in.'

Lipská smiled. 'Thank you, young man. How sensible! Now, please come in and sit down.'

Jerneková gasped. There was not a great deal of furniture, but she had never seen so many photographs. They were nearly all monochrome portraits, the majority showing someone gazing ecstatically into the near distance. All the portraits were signed flamboyantly, many dedicated to "Dear Lenka", "Dearest Lenka", "My dear Lenka" or "My dear friend Lenka".

'Just a few of the people I've worked with,' Lipská said airily. 'Do you know them?'

'I don't watch much television,' Jerneková replied.

'Television? These are theatre people. Some of our country's greatest actors and actresses.'

'And clowns?' Jerneková asked, pointing at a man in unmistakable clown costume.

'That,' said Lipská severely, 'is Tito Gobbi in *I Pagliacci*. Such a wonderful voice.'

'A musical, is it?'

'If I may interrupt, fascinating as this is,' Krob interposed, 'we mustn't take up any more of your time than is strictly necessary, Ms Lipská. I'm afraid we may have to give you some bad news. We've found the body of a friend of yours, Dominik Vitek.'

Lipská sank back into an armchair and covered her mouth with her hand. Her eyes filled with tears at once. *If this is an act*, thought Jerneková, *she's good*. 'No! Not dear Dominik!'

'I'm afraid so.'

'His heart, I suppose. He was always inclined to the fuller figure.'

'I wish it was. I'm sorry to say that someone had attacked him.'

'Hit him with something heavy,' Jerneková expanded, at once covering one shin with the other in case Krob kicked her.

'Oh, how horrible! Poor Dominik.' The tears came in floods now. 'It's so hard to imagine,' Lipská continued between sobs. 'He was such a kind man, do you see? One of the kindest I've ever known. Everyone liked him.'

'Clearly somebody didn't,' Jerneková objected, earning herself a look of reproof from Krob.

'But why? What harm had he done?'

'We were hoping you could help us with that,' said Krob. 'May we sit down?'

Lipská gestured to two chairs, one on each side of her.

'You see, on going through his effects we found some letters that you had written to him. I'm sure you remember what you wrote.'

'They were all very innocent,' Lipská protested. 'There was nothing improper in them.'

'Of course not. But without any knowledge of the context, it's hard for us to understand Mr Vitek's affairs.'

'Affairs?'

'Business affairs. There are a number of letters from others expressing similar sentiments to you, but no information about their context, you see.'

Lipská dabbed her eyes and took a deep breath. 'You're very young, so I don't imagine you remember me in my heyday,' she began.

'Our boss has told us about your family and the milk. He remembered the show with affection,' Jerneková explained.

'How kind of him. It is lovely to be remembered. Well, that show lasted until around the time of the Prague Spring. 1968, was it? Then the government wasn't so interested in the capitalist threat any longer, and they cancelled it. Well, of course that capitalist threat stuff was all tommy-rot anyway. But suddenly I had to look for work. The whole cast did. But people had been used to seeing us in those roles for ten years or so. They couldn't accept us as anything else. I made a couple of films in supporting roles, and then liberalisation was on us and that awful "New Wave" and … well, I'm sorry, but I didn't train as a serious actress for years to take my clothes off. I went back to the theatre and got some work, but it never paid enough for me to live in Prague and pay for hotels around the country.

'Then I remembered dear Dominik. Someone had brought me to The Ladies' Lounge as a guest and I'd met him there. So I asked him if he knew any theatre people in Prague who might give me some work, and bless him! He did. That went well for a while and we became firm friends. But, of course, younger actresses come along and there aren't that many good parts for more mature women, and life had started to become more difficult again. The Ladies' Lounge had closed by this time, but Dominik got me some work doing voice-overs for advertisements. I even recorded some announcements for the railways, would you believe? So, I have a lot to be thankful for where Dominik is concerned.'

'And what did you do for him in exchange?' Jerneková wanted to know.

'Me? For him? Nothing. He never asked. Oh, I introduced him to a few people, I suppose. And he stayed here in my flat once or twice when he couldn't go home. Nothing improper, you understand. Dominik wasn't made that way, you see, but he was a perfect gentleman anyway. He slept on that sofa over there.'

'So why do you think Mr Vitek kept your letters?' Krob asked.

'Sentiment, I suppose. And he was always an admirer of mine. Perhaps he hoped to sell them if he fell on hard times.'

CHAPTER 9

Peiperová felt a small thrill running up her spine. The hairstyle was a little different, and the colour certainly was, but the shape of the cheekbones and chin checked out. The Maria Suková that she had tracked down amidst a bevy of alternative Maria Sukovás was the same one who appeared in the photographs that had been retrieved from Vitek's safe.

Not only that, but this Maria Suková boasted a resumé that might well have placed her on the membership list of The Ladies' Lounge, if it had still been running then. After taking a good degree in economics she had worked for the Czech National Bank, working her way up to a senior position in their economic forecasting team. That was where she had been in May 1986 when the photographs were taken. After that she had been headhunted by a management consultancy and worked for a while in Switzerland before returning to Prague to lead the local office and take an early retirement. Tracking down an address for her was the next step, but perhaps Major Klinger could help there. As a major figure in the financial world, she might well have crossed his path.

'Maria Suková? And this is in connection with the Vitek case? Captain Slonský gave me a brief outline,' Klinger said.

While Klinger had long been an admirer of Navrátil's ability, he was less sure about Peiperová. He was no misogynist — he despised both sexes equally — but there was something about Peiperová's desk organisation that jarred with his own system. On the other hand she had the emotional intelligence to bring her own coffee mug so he would not need to clean one of his own if he gave her coffee. It then dawned on him that bringing a mug must mean that she expected to be offered coffee, so he did.

'Ms Suková is one of the women named in his files.'

'His files?'

'He had a safe full of files, but we're not sure why. We thought at first that he had been blackmailing them, but some of the women named have written notes to him thanking him for giving them money.'

'That would certainly be a novel approach to blackmailing people,' Klinger mused.

'So we thought if we could speak to some of them we might be able to uncover his motive in keeping those files. He had them locked in a concealed safe, so they must have been important to him.'

'I see. I can't make any promises, but I know one or two people who may have worked with her. I'll make some calls.'

'I'd be very grateful, Major.'

Hardly anyone referred to Klinger by his rank. It was good to be appreciated, he thought. He revised his opinion of Peiperová, sure in the knowledge that she would not have learned elementary courtesies working for Slonský. The thought fleetingly crossed his mind that she could be an ally in his plan to prise Navrátil away from Slonský's clutches; surely a wife would have some influence over her husband, particularly an intelligent and attractive one such as the specimen before him? This was supposition on Klinger's part. He had trouble forming long-term relationships because very few women enjoy smelling of disinfectant, but it did not worry him. He enjoyed his nights at the opera, the chess club and his walking holidays on which he took many hundreds of photographs that he never showed anybody.

When Peiperová had gone, he opened his address book and riffled through it, selecting the most likely candidate and dialling the number using the eraser on the end of his pencil.

Mucha was sitting at the table glumly forcing down a sandwich when a large shadow drifted across his face. 'Oh, it's you,' he said.

'Don't get over-excited,' Slonský replied. 'Temper your natural enthusiasm with a modicum of decorum.'

'It'll be difficult, but I'll try,' Mucha answered.

Slonský placed his plate on the table and slid a smaller one across its surface to Mucha.

'What's this?'

'A little gift from me,' Slonský told him. 'A gesture of friendship. You've been looking a bit peaky lately, so I thought you need livening up.'

'With a donut?'

'Not just a donut,' Slonský replied. 'An American donut.'

'Why would I want an American donut?'

'You're not anti-American, are you?'

'No, I'm anti-donut.'

'Have you ever had a chocolate hazelnut donut?'

'No.'

'Then how do you know you don't like it? Broaden your gastronomic horizons. Live a little.'

'I'm eating a sandwich. I won't miss these when I retire, I can tell you.'

Slonský maintained the sort of forced cheerfulness normally seen only in children's television personalities. 'You won't get American donuts at home,' he chirped.

'That's the best reason you've given me for staying there,' Mucha responded.

'That's right,' protested Slonský. 'Look a gift horse in the mouth. Reject a present from your oldest friend.'

'I don't mean — hang on, where did you get this?'

'From that little truck parked outside the entrance to the park.'

'The little brown truck?'

'That's right.'

'The one the hygiene department keep closing down?'

'Don't be melodramatic. They closed them once.'

'They did it again while you were in hospital.'

'There you are, then. How was I to know? Anyway, that was about his cooking, and he doesn't cook these.'

'Just leaves them uncovered on a fly-infested shelf.'

Slonský sighed. 'I'm trying to support a man who is doing his best to make an honest living.'

Suddenly it all became clear to Mucha. 'What did you nick him for?' he asked.

'Public nuisance. Offering women money for sex in the street.'

'Stopping women walking past to offer them cash?'

'That's right.'

'Did they accept?'

'One or two. Till they discovered he meant sex *in* the street.'

'And he's working in a public park?'

'He's harmless. He's inside a truck and they gave him some drugs when he was inside to calm his urges.'

'Suppose they wear off?'

Slonský shrugged. 'He doesn't make enough money to tempt a woman now.'

'He's made some off you, old pal.'

'No, he hasn't,' Slonský declared. 'He said I could have it for free.'

'And why would he do that?'

'Because it's one of yesterday's. He was going to throw it out.'

Navrátil turned up his collar in an attempt to make himself anonymous. He had been given an address by Věra's last employer, and was about to investigate it. He was alone, having told Krob not to tell Slonský where he was or what he was doing.

'What do I say if he asks?' Krob enquired.

'Tell him I'm at the dentist.'

'Why?'

'Why?' Navrátil repeated.

'Yes, why? He's sure to ask what the emergency was.'

'I don't know. Maybe I've lost a filling.'

'You don't have any fillings.'

'How do you know that?' Navrátil asked.

'Kristýna mentioned it last week. She said neither of you had.'

'I'm seeing my bank manager then.'

'Without your wife? He'll ask her why you're at the bank and she'll know nothing about it.'

'I'm in church praying, then!'

'That's fine. He'll buy that.'

As Navrátil approached the door there was some truth in the statement, because he was praying that Věra would still be living there. The doorbell echoed inside the flat as if it might be empty, but after a moment or two a figure could be seen approaching through the frosted glass that allowed a little light into the hallway.

'Yes?' Věra barked. 'Oh, it's you. Jan, isn't it?'

'That's right, Mrs Slonská.'

'Call me Věra. You'd best come in.'

'Thank you.'

Navrátil wiped his feet so as not to stain the carpet, a gesture that might have had more point if there had been a carpet. Almost all the floor was bare, except for a small plastic mat in the kitchen in front of him and a carpet offcut in the room to his right. Věra invited him to step through.

'I don't have any coffee, I'm afraid,' she said. 'I need to go to the shops but I've been busy.'

'Job hunting?' suggested Navrátil. His voice carried a note of concern that she responded to.

'That's right.'

'Your last employer said you'd left this forwarding address. You've just moved here.'

'That's right too. Not quite settled yet.' She waved an arm about her as if conjuring up furniture, hinting that it might still be in store.

'I'm sorry. Things must be difficult.'

'I get by,' she said defiantly.

'I'm sure you do. I gather they had to reduce their staff a bit.'

'They lost an office cleaning contract. Didn't need so many of us. Couldn't pay us if we stayed. It's pretty well just family members there now. A bit of a bolt from the blue, though. Thursday, you're polishing the brass signs outside an office, Friday, they're putting your last pay packet in your hands and giving you your slip so you can sign on for benefits.'

'I'm sorry. I don't know what to say.'

'Don't say anything. Especially not to that boss of yours. He'll be crowing over it if he hears.'

'He isn't like that.'

'Remember I was married to him. Still am, come to think of it.'

Navrátil reflected that he had now been with Slonský longer than Věra had lived with him and might well have known him better than she did, but thought it would have been inappropriate to make that point. 'I'm afraid I'm here on business,' Navrátil remarked, reminding himself that Věra was on the list of persons of interest in the killing of Dominik Vitek, so he ought not to be too friendly with her.

'Police business?'

'Yes. Someone has been killed and the police have a file on him. Your name is in it.'

'Mine? Why?'

'I don't know. I was hoping you could tell me.'

Věra shook her head as if trying to make it all go away. 'Well, who is it?'

'A man called Dominik Vitek.'

'I've never heard of him.'

'You're sure?'

'His name doesn't ring any bells at all.'

'It must be some time ago. It's an StB file.'

Věra was visibly shocked. 'The StB had a file on me?'

Strictly speaking, no, thought Navrátil, *but let her think that if it concentrates her mind.* 'You're described as one of Vitek's associates.'

'I've no idea why. I told you, I don't know the man. Didn't know the man,' she corrected herself.

'You didn't work for him?'

'Not that I know of. I worked for a lot of people as an agency cleaner or waitress. But why would they bother about one of those?'

'Perhaps because of whom you were married to?' Navrátil suggested.

'Josef?' Věra laughed. 'We were together for two years. I had a marriage and a good job, and I go and throw it all away by running off with someone who didn't actually love me. It took me ages to get a job again without the proper papers. A job that didn't involve cash in hand, nothing said, just get exploited because you can't argue or you'll have nothing. What kind of fool was I? And you can tell your boss that when you see him. Maybe it's what he wants to hear.'

Navrátil stood. He wanted to encourage her to try once more with Slonský, but she was a potential suspect in a murder enquiry. Now was not the time. 'It's his business and yours, not mine,' he said quietly. 'But I know him well enough to know he wouldn't have married a fool. I'll see myself out.'

Navrátil was writing up his notes from the interview when the office door opened. He quickly slid the sheet into the file in case it was Slonský, then relaxed when his wife's face appeared.

'Major Klinger has found a telephone number for Maria Suková. I've made an appointment to see her in an hour. Do you want to come?' Peiperová asked.

'I'm sure you can handle it.'

'Yes, but it's your case. I thought I should run it past you.'

Navrátil laid his pen down carefully. 'I don't expect you to stop using your initiative just because I'm nominally in charge, just as I'm sure you'd reciprocate when you're in charge.'

'I'll let you know if that happens. I haven't led an inquiry yet.'

'You will.'

'Will I? Or are you the blue-eyed boy of the moment?'

'Please don't get jealous. It doesn't suit you. We're a team. We work together.'

'Only because you say so. You could stop saying so.'

'You know me better than that.'

Peiperová turned away and breathed an exaggerated sigh before slapping the doorjamb and turning back. 'Sorry. It just got to me for a moment.'

'No problem. Just trust me. I won't work against your interests. Your interests are my interests.'

Peiperová leaned over the desk. 'Would it be very unprofessional to kiss you?'

'Of course it would. We're at work.'

'Would you report me for it?'

'No. Because I'd be equally guilty and you might report —' The sentence went unfinished as she effectively closed his mouth with her own.

'Let that be a lesson to you,' she said. 'I'll let you know how I get on with Suková.'

'Fine. Are you taking Lucie?'

'If I do, she'll want to drive.'

'That'll be a no, then.'

Sergeant Voyta shuddered when he saw the two women approaching.

'Lucky I came back from the toilets when I did,' said Jerneková, 'or you might have had to go without me.'

'Isn't it?' Peiperová replied, still unsure where she had gone wrong in the conversation that landed her in this mess.

'Good afternoon, Sergeant,' said Jerneková. 'Just a small car, please.'

Voyta was in charge of the car pool, a collection of motor vehicles that was beginning to look a little thin since some of the cars had been sent to the body shop to get dents hammered out. 'I'm not sure we've got anything suitable,' Voyta said, gazing across the yard. 'Are you driving?'

'Of course,' said Jerneková.

Voyta eased himself out of the little heated hut that surrounded him. It was snug enough to have been made to measure. 'Are you going far?'

'Just across the city,' Peiperová replied. 'Out to the west. No convenient tram, unfortunately.' She hoped that the edge in her voice had not been detectable.

'How about this one?' asked Voyta.

'It's already got a dent in it,' Jerneková pointed out.

'That'll save you some trouble then,' Voyta replied, then felt a slight bolt of fear as he realised that Peiperová was a superior officer, but she had turned away as if she had not heard the remark, though, if she had not, why was she smirking?

A few minutes later Jerneková was pulling into the Prague traffic. 'What's he honking for? I was signalling.'

'Your use of signals is much improved,' Peiperová told her. 'Stopping at give way lines, not so much.'

'Whatever happened to ladies first? Hang on, I need to get over to the right-hand lane.'

'Wait till the next river crossing. You can't get across in time for this one.'

'Wanna bet?'

Peiperová was not a religious woman, but a prayer flew to her lips in no time as Jerneková made the manoeuvre.

'That was tight,' Jerneková announced as she nudged in front of a startled cyclist.

'It was, wasn't it,' Peiperová agreed. 'Maybe next time you'll listen to me and not turn right from the centre lane.'

'Noted.'

'You want the next left. But give way first.'

The rest of the journey was quite uneventful, at least by Jerneková's standards, if you disregarded the delivery driver jumping back behind his van and the game of chicken with the tram driver.

They pulled up reasonably close to the kerb, at least at the front, and the two officers stepped out.

'Not bad,' Jerneková declared with a low whistle. 'I wonder what an apartment in this district costs.'

'We'll never know. And this isn't an apartment building. Suková owns the whole thing.'

'She's done all right for herself, hasn't she? I went to a high school that was smaller than this.'

A man pushing a wheelbarrow touched his cap to them as they walked along the path to the front door. Peiperová rang the bell, which was answered by an elegant woman of about sixty in an expensively tailored navy trouser suit.

'You must be the detectives,' Maria Suková said. 'Do come in, though I can't imagine what you want with me. Go through on the left and I'll bring us some coffee.'

They sat on a sofa covered in ivory striped fabric.

'Do you think you can go round here on public holidays?' Jerneková whispered.

'I doubt it. It's her home.'

'There must be money in being an ecologist.'

'Economist. She's a specialist in finance.'

'Yeah, looks like it.' Jerneková indicated the fireside rug. 'Do you think she shot that herself?'

Peiperová leant over to run her hand over it. 'I doubt it. It's synthetic.'

Suková appeared with a tray and poured the coffees. 'Sugar?' she asked.

'No, thanks,' Jerneková answered. 'I'm sweet enough.'

Peiperová suffered a short spasm of coughing.

'Now,' Suková said, 'to business. You said you have some questions for me.'

'Yes,' said Peiperová, reaching into her bag for a folder which she perched on the end of the sofa. 'I have to tell you that a man was recently found dead in his flat whom we believe you knew.'

'Indeed?'

'A man named Dominik Vitek.'

'I did know him. It's been some years since we spoke.'

'Did you fall out?' Jerneková butted in.

'No. Just didn't see much of each other. Vitek retired and apart from an occasional wave across a crowded foyer at the theatre that was about the end of our interaction. How did he die?'

'Someone bashed —' Jerneková began.

'We suspect foul play,' Peiperová interrupted loudly.

'How awful. He was a good man,' Suková told them.

'What makes you say that?' Jerneková asked.

'The fact that it's true. He was a great help to me when I was younger.'

Peiperová opened the folder and found the sheet she wanted. 'He had a number of folders relating to women. But only women.'

'He was an ally, long before we used the word. No doubt you've heard about The Ladies' Lounge.'

'Yes, we have. You were a member, I believe.'

'I was a committee member for a while. We ran it as a private club. Guests had to be signed in and the committee vetted all applications for membership. You young women can't imagine what it was like to have a safe place to go back then. It kept us sane, back when a woman couldn't just go anywhere. You'd get groped by drunks, and not so drunks. My bottom has been pinched or slapped so many times. It's better now.'

'Your bottom?' Jerneková enquired.

'Women's rights. I'm not pretending it never happens, but you can go around town and not get any unwanted attention from men.'

'Tell me about it,' said Jerneková.

'The point is,' Peiperová said, a little louder than she intended, 'that we need to find out why those folders existed. This is a copy of yours.'

'A copy?' Suková said.

'The original is being examined forensically.'

'I see.'

'There's not much in the folder, but there is a hotel receipt and these photographs.' Peiperová passed it to Suková who glanced at it briefly before handing it back.

'Just these photographs?' she asked.

'Just these three.'

'I see.'

Jerneková could not restrain herself. 'There were others, weren't there?' she asked.

Suková pushed her spectacles up her nose and her eyes flicked away briefly. 'Yes,' she said.

CHAPTER 10

'Would you like to tell us about it?' Peiperová prompted.

'Not really, but I suppose you need to know. However, I would appreciate some discretion.'

'Discretion is our middle name,' Jerneková replied. Peiperová produced an involuntary eye roll.

'It was in the mid-Eighties, I think.'

'The receipt is dated 1986,' Peiperová interrupted. 'I assume the receipt and the photographs belong together.'

'Yes. I would have been thirty-eight, I suppose. Married to a man I met at university. He was a top official in the ministry of heavy industry. Going places — so was I, in my own quieter way. He spent a lot of time away from home. Drank too much. Always obsessing about conspiracies to ease him out of his job. Difficult to live with, you see. I didn't mind at first. I had my own career to forge, connections to make. I didn't want to get promotions just because I was his wife. People were beginning to hint that was why I was getting on so well. Nothing to do with being the star student at university and head of my own department at thirty-five.'

Maria Suková paused for a sip of coffee. 'There was a young man. An intern, very clever and competent. He showed an interest. We went to a conference and things happened that shouldn't have, and they carried on after we got back. Maybe we got careless, but we certainly were entrapped. One afternoon we met at a hotel and it seems someone took some pictures.'

'Like the one I've just shown you?' Peiperová interjected.

'No, that's pretty innocent, isn't it? Just a couple of people whose profiles you can barely see walking towards the elevators. But when we asked for a room the desk clerk gave us a small conference room. Room 305. I can still remember that. Funny, isn't it? The things that stick in your mind. There was a sofa but no bed, but we didn't need one, and in our eyes that would just demonstrate to others the innocence of our meeting. There must have been a camera concealed in the room somewhere. We'd drawn the curtains in case anyone could see us from the buildings opposite. Anyway, there were half a dozen photos that I saw. They left nothing to the imagination. You could see our faces and a lot more beside. I couldn't deny it was me.' Suková stopped and stood abruptly. 'I could do with a glass of wine. Can I offer you one?'

'Ye—' Jerneková began.

'We're working,' Peiperová announced loudly, 'but don't let us stop you.'

Suková returned with a large glass of red wine. Her hand trembled as she tried to drink from it and she had to steady it with her other one. 'I was sent the photos.'

'At home, or at work?' Peiperová asked.

'At work. It came with a note saying they wanted a huge sum in US dollars or Deutschmarks in exchange for not sending the photos to my husband. He'd have divorced me and got me sacked.'

'He might not,' Peiperová commented. 'The sacking, I mean.'

'You don't know Tomáš. Anything that could bring him down had to be discarded. My ability wouldn't have saved me. He was senior enough to tell my boss to get rid of me. But I had no idea where to get that kind of money. People used to think there was hard Western currency lying around at the economics ministry. We spent half our time trying to do swap deals precisely because we didn't have Western money. I was beside myself. I gave serious thought to ending it all.'

Jerneková uttered an exclamation. 'Sorry,' she said. 'Shouldn't have said that. I meant "Wow".'

'I went to see Dominik. Well, that's not quite right. I went to The Ladies' Lounge to get smashed. Dominik saw me sitting at the bar with my fourth or fifth drink in my hand and black mascara on my cheeks, and took me into his private office. I told him what had happened. He told me to let him think about it for a day or two and put me in a taxi to go home. I was off work for a couple of days with a migraine. The stress was incredible. Then I got a phone call from Dominik. He invited me to go to his office. He had the photos. He'd bought them from the blackmailers, bless him. I don't know where he got the money. I said I'd pay him back. He said I couldn't. I'd never earn enough to be able to divert sufficient without my husband noticing. In any event, he said, he'd taken steps to protect his interests. A few days later he had the money back. Apparently it had been rescued from a wrecked car in which a couple of men were killed. I'm not a fool; I can imagine Dominik knew people who could arrange that sort of accident. Anyway, I didn't want the photos and I thought Dominik had destroyed them all. Obviously not. There were just these three?'

'Just these three,' Peiperová confirmed.

'I wish I knew what had happened to the others. Not that I need to worry now, I suppose. I'm twenty-three years older, and Tomáš and I got divorced anyway. My choice. When the Wall came down and he lost his position he stopped being a pompous, overbearing drunk and became a needy, whiny drunk. I prospered, he didn't.'

'And Vitek never asked for any sort of payback for what he did?' asked Peiperová.

'Never. Even when times became difficult he didn't try to call in a favour. I did help him voluntarily once, when he needed finance in a hurry and I arranged a commercial loan for him, but there was nothing untoward about it. I just knew some people who wouldn't take advantage of him. But that must have been about ten years later.'

'And you haven't seen or spoken to him lately?'

'No, not lately. About four years ago we had a quick chat at the ballet during the interval.' She smiled.

'Something amusing?' Peiperová asked.

'I squeezed his arm, just as a sort of thank you, to show I hadn't forgotten his kindness, and he patted me on the hand and said, "We girls have to stick together, you know!" and winked at me. That was the last I saw of him.'

'Thank you. I'll have to ask you to give us a formal statement in due course, but I think we can gloss over some of the detail you've given us.'

The detectives picked up their bags and made for the door.

'Thank you,' said Suková. 'I'd be grateful. Do you know when the funeral will be? I'd like to pay my respects to him.'

'When I find out I'll let you know. By the way, he didn't have any family that you know of?' Peiperová asked.

'Sorry, I don't know. I don't think anyone was ever mentioned.'

'What about partners?' Jerneková chipped in.

'Dominik had a lot of friends, but no long-term relationships while I knew him. He liked to play to the circle, you see.'

Navrátil was giving Krob and Slonský an update, carefully omitting any mention of one name on the list of those to be interviewed, when Peiperová and Jerneková returned. Jerneková had a triumphant glow about her.

'Only reversed into a parking space without hitting anything,' she proudly proclaimed. 'You may applaud.'

'Yes, and so quickly,' Peiperová added.

Navrátil quickly recapped what he had learned so far, and invited Peiperová to report on the interview with Maria Suková.

'I'm not sure it gets us very far,' she said. 'She confirms that she knew Dominik Vitek but had not seen him lately. In 1986 she was the subject of a blackmail attempt involving photographs covertly taken in a Prague hotel of an encounter with a young male intern. The photographs we've seen are from that occasion, but there were more explicit ones.'

'I wish I'd seen those,' Jerneková interrupted, then, realising that everyone was looking at her in an accusatory way, she said, 'so that we could judge whether she was entitled to be so worried about them getting out.'

'Vitek took care of it for her,' Peiperová continued. 'Allegedly he bought the photos, then got his money back when the blackmailers had a car accident. It would be interesting to know whether there were any suspicions raised about the accident in our files.'

'Ask Mucha to see what he can dig out,' Slonský suggested.

'Anyway, Vitek seems to have destroyed the other photos.'

'But he kept these. I wonder why?' asked Slonský.

'Souvenir? Reminder of a good deed?' Peiperová suggested.

'And you think she was genuine?' Slonský enquired.

'I think so. She was reluctant to tell us anything and we had to promise to be discreet with the information. She seemed really upset to have to recall it, wouldn't you say, Lucie?'

'Yes. On the verge of tears much of the time, I'd say,' Jerneková confirmed.

'Oh, I don't doubt her sincerity,' Slonský answered. 'I've no reason to. Just her accuracy.'

'Come again?' Jerneková blurted out.

'I think she's telling you the truth as she knows it, but of course it's a tissue of lies.'

'How do you make that out, sir?' Jerneková demanded.

Slonský raised an interrogative eyebrow towards Navrátil and Krob. It was the latter who spoke first.

'Who has the clout to get a hotel room set up with concealed cameras back in 1986 if not the StB?' Krob asked. 'And if it was the StB, Vitek would not have dared to interfere in their operation. He certainly wouldn't have ambushed a couple of operatives and taken the money back if there was the remotest chance that a finger would be pointed at him.'

'Good lad!' beamed Slonský. 'You win tonight's star prize.'

'Which is?' Krob wanted to know.

'There's an American donut on my desk.'

'I'll pass, thank you. I'm not into vintage patisserie.'

'Just a minute,' Peiperová interjected. 'You're saying Suková's story doesn't hang together.'

'I'm sure she believes it, perhaps because she wants to believe it. Vitek sorted out a problem for her and her relief clouded her judgement.'

'So how could he get the StB to abandon a surveillance and give him the photos?'

'How fast did he get them back?'

'A couple of days, by the sound of it.'

Jerneková nodded her agreement.

'Well, there you are,' said Slonský. 'I worked with these people. Trying to find out who was managing a case could take you more than two days, and that was if you were in the police. An outsider would have no chance. In my experience there were three ways to get the StB to drop something. You were an insider with enough rank to tell them to do it. You were an informer who gave them something juicy enough that they were prepared to trade. Or you knew who had put them up to it and you persuaded him to drop it, which probably means a bit of counter-blackmail. But that's risky, because whoever it is could put the StB on to you.'

'Vitek was StB or an StB informer?' Jerneková gasped. 'But everyone says how nice he was.'

'Just think, lass, how much easier the life of an informer is if he can get people to think that?'

'How do we find out what Vitek was?' Navrátil asked.

'Nobody knows an informer like other informers. But it's got to be one who was around twenty years ago. Let's see if we can find Václav.'

Slonský cultivated a number of informers, but none had a longer, nor more fruitful, association with him than Václav the Storyteller. If Slonský had ever known his real name it was long forgotten, and since it was better that way he made no particular effort to recall it.

There was a time-honoured method for finding Václav. You bought a newspaper, folded it under your arm, and walked slowly round Old Town Square, paying special attention to the astronomical clock. After a few minutes of doing this you found a café in a side street and ordered a coffee. If Václav was around he would join you. You ordered a coffee and something to keep the cold out for Václav, and when you left you "forgot" your newspaper, which would have a banknote between pages one and three.

On this particular occasion Slonský and Navrátil had strolled around for a minute or two when Slonský spotted a familiar figure in a shop doorway. He tapped Navrátil on the shoulder and ostentatiously pointed out the way they should go. They sat down at a table — inside, of course — and Slonský ordered three coffees and two plum brandies. 'You won't want one,' he said.

'Not during working hours,' Navrátil pronounced primly.

'I'm only having it to keep Václav company.'

'Are you sure he's coming?'

'He's coming, lad. Just tidying himself up a bit. He'll be keen to ensure that he doesn't know anyone else here. That's why it's good to pick out-of-the-way places.' He took a sip from his cup. 'It also helps if they serve the worst coffee in town,' he added.

Navrátil tried his own and winced. 'Can you burn coffee?' he pondered.

'I'm sure you can if you try hard enough.'

The door opened and a nondescript man left over from the Seventies slipped inside. He wore a heavy woollen coat, a plaid shirt with a grubby undershirt, and boots that may once have been army issue. His head consisted of about sixty per cent grey beard and he removed a fur cap and smoothed his scalp with the flat of his hand as a substitute for combing the hair he no longer had.

'Nippy out there,' Václav remarked.

'Never mind. Got you a little something to warm you up. Have you eaten?' Slonský asked.

'I never say no. You don't know where the next meal is coming from, do you?'

'Navrátil, be an angel and ask for a couple of sandwiches. Have one yourself if you want. Tell them to add it to my tab.'

Navrátil did as he was bidden.

'How's life?' Slonský asked.

'Not so bad. Got myself a regular room now.'

'Good. You need somewhere to stow your stuff. Makes you less conspicuous.'

Václav took a sip of the spirit and smacked his lips appreciatively. 'The coffee's awful here but they keep a decent drop of the good stuff.'

'Dominik Vitek is dead.'

'So I heard.'

'The word is that he may have been an informer for the StB back in the day.'

Václav shrugged. 'Who wasn't? But I never heard that he was a regular source. If he had been, all those folks he mixed with would have been run in.'

'You mean the dissidents?' asked Navrátil.

'Well, them too. But actually I was thinking about the homosexuals.'

'Was Vitek gay?' Slonský asked.

'I don't think so. I don't think he had any real interest in that sort of thing with anyone. He was just flamboyant. Loved the stage. But one or two of those he mixed with were definitely on the other side of the bed. They must have trusted him.'

'Here's the problem. Everyone tells us how nice Vitek was, such a kind man, the sort of friend that everyone would want to have. I tell you, it's sorely testing my lack of faith in human nature.'

'He was a good sort. A genuinely funny man too, I hear.'

'I thought his cabaret ridiculed the powers that be?' put in Navrátil.

'It did,' agreed Slonský, 'but not as viciously as some. I wouldn't mind betting that the politicians he picked on tolerated him for exactly that reason. It gave the impression that they could laugh at themselves without doing them any real damage. Mind, if they'd had a sense of humour they might have understood what he was saying and been a bit less accommodating. As it was they jailed a bunch of dissidents but left Vitek at large. They niggled him a bit, took him in for questioning once or twice just to remind him not to go too far, but he kept his fingernails.'

'I tell you who would be worth asking,' Václav said suddenly. 'Jakub Petrák.'

'Is that old scoundrel still alive? Where would I find him?'

'He's in a nursing home in Slivenec, I believe. He worked for Vitek back in the day. I don't know the address, I'm afraid, but I'm sure a detective of your ability can find him.'

'I'm sure I can. But I'll let Navrátil do it. He needs the practice.'

'Right,' announced Slonský. 'You can drive.'

'Where are we going, sir?' Navrátil asked.

'Slivenec, of course.'

'Shouldn't we check his address first?'

'Where's the fun in that? There can't be many nursing homes in a place like Slivenec. It's a sort of ensuite bathroom for Prague. But if you insist, nip inside and ask Mucha while I butter up Sergeant Voyta to give us a car Jerneková hasn't wrecked.'

Voyta was pleased to see Slonský. 'That girl of yours…' he began.

'I have two. And they like to call themselves women. Calling them girls is regarded as demeaning language. Haven't you been on that course yet?'

'I don't get put on too many courses, sir, on account of running a car pool doesn't seem to call for much in the way of training.'

'Point taken. Fancy a job swap? Anyway, what were you going to say?'

'Is there any chance your assistant could learn to drive in a civilian driving school? She's costing us a fortune at the panel-beaters.'

'If she doesn't practise she won't get better.'

'Maybe central Prague isn't the best place to learn to drive. Perhaps she'd do better somewhere more open. The Great Hungarian Plain comes to mind.'

'What have the Hungarians done to upset you? I'll have a word with her and ask her to aim the car more carefully.'

Navrátil joined them. 'Mucha found an address,' he said.

'Very good, lad. If Sergeant Voyta can find us a vehicle that has a sporting chance of keeping going for forty kilometres we're set up.'

Voyta dangled some keys in the air which Slonský grabbed and lobbed to Navrátil.

'I've promised him you're a better driver than Jerneková,' Slonský said, before adding sotto voce, 'though God knows that wouldn't be hard.'

'It's the blue Fabia over there,' Voyta called to them.

'Isn't that the one Jerneková drove last week?' Slonský asked.

'That's right,' said Voyta. 'See if you can hit the offside wing to even it up.'

CHAPTER 11

Navrátil was a cautious and considerate driver, and therefore utterly unsuited to driving in Prague. It took nearly forty minutes for him to drive twenty kilometres to Slivenec, including a prolonged wait at a right turn for someone to be kind and let him into the traffic.

'Just put your foot down and keep edging forward,' Slonský advised. 'They'll soon give way. And if they don't we'll show our badges and book them.'

'We promised Sergeant Voyta we wouldn't dent the car,' Navrátil replied.

'And we won't. But we can't be held responsible for other people denting the car. I'm just getting a bit nervous that my contract is up on 11th November and I need to be back in the office by then.'

'That's months away, sir.'

'Yes, but we've still got to do the return journey. Look, there's a gap there. Pull out and straddle those two lanes.'

'I'll block the traffic.'

'Good. It'll make it easier to make the left turn up ahead.'

'It's a bit anti-social.'

'Navrátil, is this the kind of thing you mention to your priest at Confession? "Forgive me, Father, I blocked a lane trying to get across the traffic to turn left." Just say the right sort of prayer and get on with it. God will forgive you. That's his job.'

Navrátil finally managed to squeeze the car into a gap, just in time for the traffic signal to turn red.

'I only hope Petrák lives long enough for us to get there,' Slonský murmured.

The lights changed and Navrátil cautiously made the turn, keeping an eye peeled for anyone jumping the red light. Fortunately only one car did so, but in crossing the line and having to brake violently he blocked Navrátil's exit from the junction.

'Look at that!' he exclaimed to nobody in particular, because Slonský had flung the passenger door open and was striding across to speak to the offending driver. Slonský flashed his identification, thumped on the roof and told the driver that he wasn't going to book him this time because he had an aversion to paperwork and traffic duty was not his province.

'Your card says detective,' moaned the driver. 'Haven't you got any real crime to detect?'

'I specialise in homicide,' Slonský replied, 'and I can feel one coming on.'

The traffic moved, and the driver took off, leaving Slonský to stomp back to the car, pausing only to abuse the drivers behind Navrátil, who in turn were abusing him for sitting in a junction with a door open.

'I sometimes think it would be better if we just sent every Prague driver a ticket once a year on the grounds that they're sure to have done something,' Slonský growled. 'That's put me in a bad mood. If you spot a bakery pull over, lad. I need to get my blood sugar up.'

One is never very far from a bakery in Prague, and Slonský's diligent research over many years ensured that he knew nearly all of them, so he was soon able to direct Navrátil to one. 'You'll be all right, lad. There are no left turns on the route.'

'I'm perfectly capable of making a left turn, sir, provided all the other drivers obey the rules of the road.'

'You expect Prague drivers to obey the traffic laws? That's like an Inuit saying he'll grow tomatoes if it stops snowing.

Look, there's a bakery on the right. Pull up at the bus stop. I'll only be a minute.'

Slonský was true to his word, more or less, because he entered the bakery and was soon back outside, empty-handed. 'Have you got any cash, Navrátil? I must have left my wallet in my desk.'

Navrátil produced a note and Slonský trotted back inside, emerging with a large brown bag.

'That must be two hundred crowns I owe you,' Slonský said between mouthfuls of pastry.

'Three hundred and ten, actually, sir.'

'Really? I'll settle up when we get back. With inflation being what it is, by the time you get us back to the office that'll be about an hour's pay. Have you got any change? The smallest I've got in my wallet is fifty crowns.'

'Haven't you got change from that hundred I just gave you?'

Slonský looked bemused. 'Of course not. I told her to put a hundred crowns' worth of pastries in a bag. We're on a case. We haven't got time to faff around.'

'She might have given you something you don't like.'

'A pastry I don't like? Now there's a challenging idea.'

They rumbled along at a little over walking pace before the bulk of the traffic turned to the west and Navrátil was able to put his foot down.

'Which way now, sir?'

'You're the one with the address.'

'You were holding it when we left.'

'Was I?' Slonský patted each of his pockets, and finally decided to seek consolation for his loss in another pastry. 'Ah, here it is in the bag! You want to turn right past that group of trees up ahead.'

Navrátil did so.

'I meant the big group, not the little group. Never mind, second on the left and we'll be good.'

'Are we close now?' Navrátil asked, slowing to look at every building on the road.

'It must be on your side. How about we stop at that nursing home and ask for directions?'

Navrátil pulled in and parked.

'Well, that was fun,' Slonský announced, tossing the brown bag into the back seat and collecting his hat.

Jakub Petrák was in the day room watching two old men playing dominoes when the detectives entered. He had lost a lot of weight, Slonský thought, and used a wheelchair so his leg muscles were wasted. He wore a large cherry-red cardigan that swamped him so abundantly that he had gathered the surplus wool in front of him, giving him the appearance of a tired parrot on an oversized perch.

'How are you, Jakub?' Slonský asked.

Petrák told him to go away, or words to that effect.

'Are you so welcoming to all your guests?'

'Only the bastards,' Petrák growled.

Slonský patted his jacket pocket. 'I come bearing gifts. And much more useful ones than gold, frankincense and myrrh.'

Petrák glanced upwards and licked his thin lips, which were an unappealing purple colour. 'Have you found religion then?'

'No, but young Navrátil here knows where to find it if I ever want it.'

Petrák looked the younger detective up and down. 'Jesus Maria! Have his balls dropped yet?'

'I don't know, but he must have some to work with me.'

Petrák laughed in spite of himself. 'That's true. Nobody else could stomach you. Except that soft one — what was his name?'

'Lukas.'

'That's the one. What's he doing now?'

'Running the internal investigations department, keeping us all on the straight and narrow.'

'Tell him he's peeing up a waterfall. It can't be done.'

'Let's find somewhere quieter for a chat.'

'At least you won't be able to claim I jumped out of the chair and assaulted you,' Petrák announced. 'My room. Room 15. Can the lad give me a push?'

Navrátil steered the chair through the door. 'Which way, Mr Petrák?'

'Mr Petrák? Jesus, they're breeding them polite these days. To the right, son, then the second corridor on the right.'

'I'll go ahead and open the door,' Slonský told him. 'Room 15, you say?'

'You'll need the key,' Petrák snapped. 'Round my neck.'

'You lock your doors in here?' Slonský asked. 'Has anyone got anything worth nicking?'

'No, but when nobody has much you'd be surprised what becomes valuable. A disposable lighter, a few coppers, a good pair of nail clippers.'

Slonský produced a half-bottle of pear brandy from his inside pocket. 'Best lock that away then.'

Petrák held it close to his face to read the label.

'Haven't you got any spectacles?' Slonský demanded.

'Not a big one for reading,' Petrák replied. 'Nice looking drop. Thanks. I might just have a splash now to check it's not poisoned.'

'It would be a bit pointless to poison it when we want to pick your brains.'

'Figure of speech. I haven't got any glasses or I'd give you a tot.'

'That's all right. We don't drink on duty.'

Navrátil's eyes opened wide, but he decided this was not the time to produce any of the abundant evidence to the contrary.

'You take the chair,' Petrák said. 'The kid can sit on the end of the bed.' He span the cap off the bottle with a sharp flick and raised it to his lips. The spirit made him cough as it went down, but he smacked his lips in appreciation. 'Don't get many treats what with having no family.'

'Your wife leave you, then?'

'Don't know exactly. She stopped visiting when I was inside one time and when I got out she'd moved and taken the kids with her.'

'You've got children?' Navrátil enquired.

'Two.'

'And you don't see them?'

'They'll be adults now. Thought my daughter might have tried to find me, but no such luck. Probably scared she'd get hit for the care bills.'

'Would you like to find them?' Navrátil persisted.

Petrák eyed him suspiciously. 'It'd be good to know they're okay,' he mumbled. 'Looking after themselves. Maybe got kids themselves by now. If I've got grandchildren I'd want to know before I peg out.' He thumped his chest. 'Asbestos, they say. Not in great shape. I used to be able to bench press two hundred and fifty kilos, you know. Now I can't even get my own arse out of the chair.'

'You used to work for Dominik Vitek, I'm told,' Slonský said.

'That's right.'

'Someone's topped him.'

Petrák's eyes displayed a certain amount of shock. 'Vitek? Why? I mean, twenty years ago I could understand it. I might have done it myself once or twice. But he must be retired by now, surely?'

'Retired, but with a safe full of secrets. A load of files, nearly all about women. But they don't make a lot of sense without the background stories. I thought you might be able to tell us a bit about them.'

Petrák took another slurp and wiped his mouth with his sleeve. 'He was a soft one too. He'd help anyone if he could, even the ones who didn't deserve it. He used to say what comes around goes around. Everyone needs help up a ladder, he'd say.'

'So what did he do that riled you?'

Petrák gave a wheezy laugh. 'Just being himself. He'd help some basket case and I'd say, "You know there's nothing in this for you" and he'd just shrug and say, "You don't know that, Jakub. She's in the ditch now, but in ten years she could be married to someone important." The irritating bit is that often he was right. Well, if not married, at least shacked up with someone who could do him a favour.'

'Can you give me an example?'

Petrák rubbed his chin. 'I can see her face… Ditka something or other.'

Navrátil took a sheet of paper from his pocket and quickly scanned it. 'Ditka Hrubešová?' he asked.

'That's the one! She was an actress. Not a sort of National Theatre actress, more your hanging-around-in-a-bikini-in-a-cheap-movie kind. She got involved with a film director and he got her up the duff then dumped her. Someone brought her to Vitek to see if he could help. She didn't want an abortion, didn't believe in it, so he got her a room with an old actress friend of his and she worked for her keep as a sort of maid. But Vitek said he didn't want the same thing to happen to anyone else so he called me over and said, "Jakub, take Honza and pay him a visit, and take a couple of good-sized bricks with you." So Honza and I caught up with this director one evening when he'd had a skinful. Just as well, I suppose. Might have been a bit of an anaesthetic for him when we gave him an informal vasectomy with a box-cutter. Anyway, lo and behold a little while later Ditka was tucked up in a little flat by the castle, nice and handy for her new gentleman friend to visit, and some of his pillow talk was very useful for Vitek.'

'The only thing in Ms Hrubešová's file is an address,' Navrátil said. 'That and a number on a slip of paper.'

Petrák chuckled. 'The address is probably where the baby was sent. And the number will be a deposit box somewhere. He scattered them around to make it less likely that anyone could grab the lot.'

'He was blackmailing Ditka?' Navrátil said.

'No, no point. She didn't have any cash worth talking of and she'd tell him anything he wanted anyway. It'll be her politician boyfriend. There'll be some film or photos of him in action, and not the sort of snaps he'd want his mates to see. Just in case Vitek needed it, you see.' He chuckled. 'He had some film of a party bigwig back in the day. Chest full of medals, hung like a dormouse. His boyfriend was much more impressive.'

'Take a look at Navrátil's list. See if any names ring a bell,' Slonský suggested.

'He'll have to read them to me,' Petrák replied.

Navrátil began reading the names, to each of which Petrák would respond with a shake of the head.

'Hang on, backtrack a bit. Zdenka someone.'

'Zdenka Pálková?'

'Had a flower shop near a cemetery. Nice little earner, but then the council revoked her licence and someone offered her a pittance for her lease. Vitek went to see some city official who had signed the revocation and took me along. Passed me off as his "legal adviser". Anyway, the official realised there'd been a clerical error once Vitek played him a tape recording of him mouthing off about the local party secretary. Couldn't sign a new licence fast enough, especially when Vitek told him if he didn't sign it now he wouldn't be able to in ten minutes after I'd broken his fingers. All a terrible misunderstanding, according to the guy, these things happen when you're busy. So Vitek smiles and says, "We can see to it that you'll never be busy again, if you like? And if Ms Pálková is harassed again, you'll have plenty of time on your hands once I send that tape in." It did the trick.'

'But, not being rude to Ms Pálková, she's just a flower shop owner. Why did Vitek involve himself?' Navrátil wanted to know.

'Exactly my point. But he said that you never know where someone is headed. You win some, you lose some.' Petrák helped himself to another large slug from the bottle. 'I'll tell you another thing,' he said, waving his index finger to emphasise the point, 'women are different.'

'I've noticed,' said Slonský, 'but we'd best keep it to ourselves. I don't want to spoil the lad's innocence.'

'I don't mean that. I mean the way they look after each other. That lounge of his, for example. Women would tell each other what was going on and they'd do what they could to help out. You offer to do something for a bloke for nothing and he gets suspicious, wonders what you're after.'

'What sort of help?' Navrátil asked.

'Arranging childcare, helping them find a maid, giving each other lifts. Or sometimes it would be about doctors they could trust, lawyers who would help, that sort of thing. I remember one woman who'd been beaten up during a burglary. She went to your lot, but they weren't interested. They said there was no sign of a break-in so she must have let the man in herself, so it was a domestic and they didn't need to get involved. She found a woman lawyer who proved that the building manager had been bribed to lend his master key to the burglar. She still couldn't get the case reopened, but some woman whose husband was high up in the police then heard about it and talked him into doing the right thing. I drove Vitek and the woman to the railway station to see the building manager off to his new job in the back end of Moravia. Damn lucky that was all he got.'

'What about the burglar?' Slonský asked.

'Went inside for a couple of years for something he didn't do.'

'How do you know he didn't do it?' Navrátil enquired.

'Because I knew who did, and it wasn't him.'

Slonský leaned forward in his chair. 'Keep going with that list of names, Navrátil. Let's see if any more of them spur Mr Petrák's memory.'

Navrátil dutifully intoned a few more names like a schoolteacher reading the attendance register.

'That one!' Petrák interrupted. 'Morusová, Anežka. I knew her. Wrote poetry and plays. She sailed close to the wind with some of it but her brother was something in the Communist Party. She used to say she wasn't criticising the Party, just the idiots that ran it, but she knew what she was doing.'

'You say you knew her?'

'Died a while back in a house fire. They reckon she nodded off and her blanket slipped into the open fire.'

'Check it out, Navrátil. And see if you can find out who her brother is.' Too late, Slonský remembered that it was Navrátil's case, so he added lamely, 'That is, that's what I'd recommend. But of course it's up to you.'

They ran through the rest of the list but Petrák showed no recognition of any of the remaining names.

'Well, if anything comes back to you, you know where to find me,' Slonský said. 'Us, I mean. Navrátil really, it being his case.'

'I'll give it my best attention,' Petrák replied. 'Thanks for the medicine. So they made you a captain, then?'

'That's right.'

'All the competition in pokey, are they?'

Slonský slapped his hat back on his head. 'I've outlasted nearly all of them,' he said. 'There's just Lukas and Mucha from my vintage still in harness. And Mucha plans to retire soon.'

'I don't think I know him,' Petrák answered.

'Best rush to get yourself arrested then, while he's still around to book you in.'

'No, thanks. I've spent enough time in cells. This is more comfortable. Just.'

CHAPTER 12

When they arrived back at police headquarters there was a note attached to Slonský's monitor: *Please come to my office as soon as possible. Rajka.*

Slonský had seen enough of these over the years for his first reaction to be to review his actions of the last few days hurriedly, just to be sure that everything he had done had been strictly by the book; or, at least, within the spirit of the book, if not the letter; or, at least, not directly contradicting it while witnesses were around, anyway.

Believing his conscience to be quite clear he hung up his coat and hat, smoothed down his jacket, polished each shoe in turn on the back of his trouser leg, tightened the knot of his tie and strode along the corridor, down the stairs, across the foyer and into the executive corridor. The linoleum gave way to carpet, there was the exotic fragrance of young secretaries lingering in the air, and one of Dumpy Anna's staff was pushing a trolley of coffee and snacks from doorway to doorway. This was of no interest to Colonel Rajka, who subsisted on green tea and a diet that, so far as Slonský could make out, was comprised of vegetation and skinless chicken. Rajka carried a small bag of nuts in lieu of any sugary snacks, and no doubt cracked the shells in the crook of his elbow with a single twitch of his enormous biceps. Somehow Rajka was able to sit at his desk without creasing his shirt, which always looked as if it was worn once and then replaced, and, even more impressively, the top of his desk was clear except for the document he was commenting on, making careful annotations in the margin with his fountain pen.

'Take a seat,' said Rajka without looking up.

'Thank you, sir,' Slonský automatically replied. A little politeness is never a bad move when you're about to get a dressing down, he thought.

Rajka put the cap back on his pen and laid it carefully on the page to mark his place. 'I gather you've put Navrátil in charge of the Vitek case.'

Admit nothing, thought Slonský, *until you know which way the wind is blowing.* 'Under my supervision,' he said.

'He's a very promising officer,' Rajka replied. 'The experience will be good for him.'

'That's what I thought,' Slonský said, reasoning that you can't be hauled over the coals for agreeing with your boss.

'That means that you can be spared,' Rajka continued smoothly.

Damn, I didn't see that coming, thought Slonský. *This sounds like more work.*

'There's a conference in Bratislava the day after tomorrow about co-operation between a number of sections of the Czech and Slovak police forces. It's a regular thing, small numbers. Unfortunately I can't go. But we have just ascertained that you can. And as my right-hand man, who could be more appropriate? The train takes over four hours, so you'll have to travel tomorrow and stay in a hotel. My secretary has all the details.'

Although stunned by this unexpected development, Slonský had the wit to whisper, 'Expenses?'

'The hotel is billing us directly and dinner and breakfast are included. Your train ticket will be in the folder my secretary will give you, along with the agenda and the background papers. I'm sorry that you don't have long to read them but I didn't know until today that I'd be needed elsewhere. You won't have to say anything. Just maintain a watching brief and tell me anything I need to know.'

Slonský rose from his seat and started to stumble towards the door.

'Oh, and Slonský,' Rajka added, 'try not to start an international incident.'

The folder was altogether too thick for Slonský's liking. He sat at his desk, opened it and began to read. The first paper dealt with the new kit that each police force had bought, which told him, among other things, that the Czech police had taken delivery of a new helicopter — *I wonder how I can borrow that*, he wondered — whereas the Slovaks had twelve new police dogs in training. There followed a page of statistics about manpower, some information about progress towards meeting equality and diversity targets, and a summary of the graduate entry programme that was the means by which Navrátil had entered the police service. There was, he noted sadly, nothing useful like a comparison of canteen prices or a list of the nearest bars to the meeting venue. Although there was a list of attendees at the last meeting, there was no indication of those who would be attending this time. No doubt Slonský would find out when he got to the railway station just after two o'clock the next day. But that was scarcely time enough to read all these papers.

'Krob,' he said, 'read these and mark the important bits in red for me, would you?'

Navrátil had managed to find out the identity of Anežka Morusová's brother. Ivan Morus had worked in the censorship department of the Security Police, so his importance was not that he was particularly high in the hierarchy but that he had some say in what was drawn to the attention of those above him. Presumably he had managed to hide some of Anežka's writings from their gaze, but eventually something had got through.

Anežka had alleged that one of the Politburo had got a young girl pregnant. The girl in question was fifteen years old. Ordinarily, the Communist Party liked to be thought free-thinking and progressive, unhampered by bourgeois ideas of propriety, but they could be remarkably puritanical on occasion. Mistresses were fine, homosexuality was not usually a problem (for the ruling class), even graft was not an issue provided it was kept within bounds — after all, there had to be something to compensate for those long years fomenting the revolution — but anything that smacked of exploiting underage girls was not, and Anežka had been summoned to explain where she had got the information from. Navrátil had enlisted Mucha's help to track down a file on the interrogation which showed that the allegation was not denied, merely suppressed. Anežka was told what awaited her if she published the fact again. That her punishment was not more severe was down to her editor, who had done his citizen's duty by informing on her before wasting valuable paper and ink printing something that would inevitably be pulped.

Anežka had then made the mistake of visiting the girl to explain why her story had not been published, and was interrupted by the arrival of two StB men who had, according to their report, taken the girl to a psychiatric clinic and conducted Anežka home. Navrátil checked the date of their report. It was the day before she fell asleep and was burned to death. The pathologist who certified her death had noted laconically that one reason why she may not have been able to save herself was that she appeared to have tied her wrists together with twine.

The Politburo member was named in the report, at least by implication. Copies of any correspondence on the matter were to be sent to him. Navrátil had never heard of him — it must all have happened around the time that he was born — but he thought he recognised the name. Plucking his list from his inside pocket he found a woman with the same name, possibly his wife or sister. He found himself pondering the possibility that Anežka had been given the information at The Ladies' Lounge.

Mucha received the sheet of paper from Navrátil with all the enthusiasm of a vegan offered a steak tartare. 'Which one are you looking for?' he asked.

'I really want to find this woman, Helena Borská. But there's also a Vladimir Borský mixed up in this somewhere. A former Politburo member.'

'Let's start with him, then. Politburo members loved their column inches in the press. There'll be plenty about him.'

Mucha began with a newspaper search, which, to his surprise, produced very little. 'I'm not sure that "Comrade Borský visits a pig farm" is going to get you very far. Let's try government documents next.'

'I've tried papers and public files,' Navrátil said. 'I was hoping you might have access to something more enlightening.'

'He doesn't seem to have a criminal record. But he also doesn't seem to have a current residence in Prague.'

'He could be living outside the city.'

'A former Politburo member? They can't survive in the wild. Show them a dirt track and they start hyperventilating. I'd put my money on him being dead. Let's check the register of deaths.'

Considering Borský is not that common a name, there were an astonishing number of dead ones, but only two Vladimirs. One was born in 1894, while the second turned up in 1928.

'The older one would have been well into his eighties when all this happened,' Navrátil commented.

'He could still have been a Politburo member,' Mucha told him. 'They were a bunch of geriatrics. It was a moot point whether you had to resign if you died in those days. Ah, but look — the 1928 one lived in the posh part of town. Death due to heart attack, 6th March, 1992. He was sixty-three or sixty-four years old. Now, if we go back to the newspapers and check the small advertisements around then, there may be a death notice.'

'Wouldn't it come up in the search?'

'It depends how they indexed it. These days you let the computer do it all, and everything gets indexed, but when we started doing this it depended on what the indexer thought was important. I wouldn't be surprised if they only did the news pages and skipped the advertisements and notices altogether.'

It took a few minutes, but finally Mucha stabbed the screen with his index finger. 'There you are! "Borský, Vladimir, husband of Helena, sadly deceased 6th March. Funeral at the Strašnice Crematorium on Monday next at 10.15 a.m. Friends, please accept this, the only intimation." No mention of his career nor of any other family.'

'Is Helena still around?'

'She's got an ID card. It looks like she lives in an apartment block in Hostivař.'

Navrátil copied down the address. 'Thanks,' he said brightly. 'I don't know what we'll do when you're gone.'

'Celebrate, probably,' Mucha replied.

It seemed to Navrátil that, given the subject matter of the discussion, it might be better if Helena Borská was interviewed by the female members of the team, even if that meant exposing her to Lucie Jerneková's idea of appropriate small talk, so he asked Peiperová if she would try to find any additional information that would expand on the bald narrative they currently had; a writer who had been a member of The Ladies' Lounge and had fingered a Politburo member for abusing a young girl and had then died in a mysterious house fire.

'You're going to have to be tactful,' Navrátil said, his voice betraying his trepidation on this point. 'It won't be easy asking whether she knows that her husband may have fathered a child by an underage girl and then had her committed to a psychiatric institution.'

'Give me some credit,' Jerneková complained. 'I'm not stupid.'

'I'm sorry,' Navrátil stuttered, 'I didn't mean to imply…'

'Yes, you did. You were looking sideways at me when you said it.'

'I didn't need telling either,' Peiperová said, 'but better to make sure we both knew that than stumble into difficulty by making an assumption.'

Somewhat mollified, Jerneková fetched her coat. 'Anyway, she wouldn't be the first schoolgirl to be duffed and dumped,' she declared.

To Jerneková's disappointment, Peiperová had insisted on driving to Hostivař, her excuse being that she could not navigate and superintend the driving at the same time.

'Does that mean I can drive on the way back?' Jerneková asked brightly.

'I suppose so,' Peiperová conceded. Before joining the police, she had once helped a friend for a few days through a period of staff sickness at a kindergarten in Kladno, and the skills learned then were increasingly coming into play now.

They found the address and climbed the stairs, the lift being out of order. Judging by the state of the sign, it had been out of order for some time.

'It's not exactly a select area, is it?' whispered Jerneková. Despite her low voice, the echo in the stairwell meant she could have been clearly heard on the fifth floor, which was where they were headed.

'Nevertheless, it's someone's home,' Peiperová reproved her.

'Don't get me wrong, I've known worse. You should have seen my old room in Most.'

'I did,' Peiperová reminded her.

'Oh, yeah. This is better. But at least mine wasn't up several flights of stairs.'

They collected themselves at the top, breathing deeply before ringing the doorbell.

'I hope she's not out after all that,' said Jerneková.

'How could she get out with no lift?'

'She could get out. Probably wouldn't be able to get back in again though.'

The door opened and an elderly woman looked out at them suspiciously. 'You're not Mormons, are you?' she said.

'No,' Peiperová told her.

'Jehovah's Witnesses, then?'

'No. We're police.'

They held up their identification for inspection. The woman retrieved a pair of spectacles hanging round her neck on a cord and examined each one carefully, not releasing the chain and dragging Jerneková forward to bring hers into focus. 'What do you want with me?' she asked.

'A few questions about a rather delicate matter,' Peiperová answered. 'May we come in?'

'If you must.' The door chain was released and the door swung back. 'Watch your step. I've got a cat but she's not too good with the litter tray.'

The said animal was lounging across a sofa, lying on a woollen throw. Her owner removed her by tugging sharply on one corner of the throw and yanking hard, much to the cat's disgust. She landed on the floor and arched her back before heading for a basket in the corner.

'You can sit there if you like.'

Peiperová gingerly took a seat, having examined the throw for any cat-related nuisances.

'I'll stand,' Jerneková declared. 'We've been in the car a long time.'

'We're investigating the death of a man named Dominik Vitek,' Peiperová began.

'He's dead?' said Helena Borská.

'I'm afraid so. We suspect foul play.'

'I didn't know he was still alive. I haven't seen him for years, like a lot of my so-called friends back then.'

'He cut you off?'

'My husband got himself into a spot of bother. In those days people played safe. They didn't mix with "social undesirables".'

'What did he do?' asked Jerneková.

'Never you mind.'

'I think we may know, Mrs Borská,' Peiperová intervened. 'In the process of our investigation we found some files relating to The Ladies' Lounge. Were you a member?'

'Yes, years back. Anyone who was anyone was. Mind you, I'll say this for Dominik. When the fuss blew up, he didn't expel me. I just couldn't face going and looking at all their sanctimonious faces.'

'We also found a file relating to a woman called Anežka Morusová.'

'She was a good type. Came to a sticky end though.'

'She tried to publish a story about your husband, we believe.'

'No "we believe" about it, dearie. She wrote it, and it was spiked.'

'She had found out that he had fathered a child with a young girl.'

'She didn't "find out". I told her.'

'You told her?' Jerneková interrupted.

'Yes. I was mad as hell. We hadn't had children and since we'd stopped doing that kind of thing because he was always too tired I was never going to have one. Then this young bit turns up at the door hoping to speak to him.'

'She came here?' Jerneková asked.

'No, we didn't live here then. He never did. We had a nice place behind the castle in the government quarter. It was a gated compound. I couldn't think how she got in. Turned out she snuck on the end of a school party and then hid inside the gates until he came home. He'd shrugged her off but she had seen where he lived, so she came back the next day. Made up some story about losing her ID during the tour of the castle area then jumped over a fence. She rang the doorbell and I answered.'

'And she told you what had happened?' Peiperová probed gently.

'She said she didn't know where to turn. Her mum worked nights and she couldn't talk to her without her dad hearing, and he'd have killed her, she reckoned. She'd tried to speak to my husband but he wasn't having any of it, said it must be some other lad who'd done it because she was easy. Well, whatever she was she wasn't that. She was more hurt by that suggestion than anything else, I reckon.'

'I can imagine,' Peiperová nodded.

'I mean, that's the standard way men deal with troublesome women, isn't it? Deny everything. As if the poor thing got herself pregnant. Don't get me wrong, I'm not condoning what she did. But if you're fifteen and an important man pays attention to you, it's not surprising if your guard slips.'

'She told you all this?'

'Yes, the whole lurid tale. She'd been doing a gymnastics display and she'd been presented to him. He told her how pretty she looked, how talented, all that stuff. Then he suggests that after she's got changed she should come to his car and he'll take her for a meal. We had access to some things the ordinary folk couldn't get, you see. So he gets her something to eat then asks her if she's ever had a glass of wine — of course, she hadn't — and a couple of glasses later she's on the back seat of his official car and the driver's taking them on a tour of the city with the curtains drawn. A few weeks later she finds out why she's feeling rough and thinks it must be him because he's the only man she's ever been with.'

'So what did you do?'

'There wasn't a lot I could do. I didn't have much money of my own, but I gave her a bit and told her I'd talk to a friend and see what we could do for her. I didn't have anyone particular in mind but I thought Dominik might have an idea. Anyway, when I got to the Lounge Anežka was there and I blurted it all out to her. She wasn't a journalist, you see. She was a proper writer. I'd got the girl's details and when Anežka asked for them I handed them over. I thought she was going to help. I didn't realise she was going to write it all up.'

'And she went to see the girl?'

'Yes, she got the whole story and a bit of corroborating evidence. But before that I'd had it out with Vladimir. He started on about how busy he was, how he couldn't be at my beck and call, and I lost it. I said he wasn't too busy to get a fifteen-year-old in the family way. He shouted at me about it being lies. I said I knew it wasn't because I'd spoken to the girl. "She came here?" he said, and twisted my wrist. He was foaming at the mouth. Now, he couldn't go and see her because he'd had so little regard for her that he hadn't got her address, but he told me to tell him where she lived. Luckily I couldn't — I'd given the paper to Anežka, you see. It cost me a couple of cracked ribs but I didn't give her up.'

'But he found her,' Peiperová said gently.

'Got the StB onto it. Said she'd threatened him with a made-up story and that she was mentally disturbed. They took her away. I don't know what happened to her. Then the next thing I heard Anežka had been killed in a house fire. I swear to God I thought I was next. I said I wanted a divorce. He said a man in his position needed a wife, and if I behaved myself and said no more about it he would keep me on out of the goodness of his heart.'

'So you stayed?'

'I didn't have much choice. But his career didn't recover. Within a year he'd been sacked and there was no reason to stay with him. I managed to see the First Secretary's wife and cried a bit on her shoulder. I told her I was ashamed to be married to someone who had betrayed the Party as he had, and she must have had a word in the right ear, because a week or two later I was allocated a small villa. We both had to live there, but it was really two little flats in one building. We didn't get divorced but we might as well have been. I got an allowance direct from the State — which I'm pleased to say was bigger than his — and that lasted until the Wall came down. Then one day I came downstairs and he was gasping for breath in the doorway. "Call an ambulance!" he said, so I made a cup of coffee and a sandwich, then I made the call.'

'We've seen the funeral announcement,' Jerneková said.

'For public consumption. Nobody came. I didn't expect they would. They cremated him and gave me a cardboard box with his ashes in. They put his name on a plaque on a wall at the cemetery and invited me to scatter his ashes there. I didn't bother.'

'What did you do with him?' Peiperová asked.

'Flushed him down the toilet. In instalments, mind; I didn't want him to block it.'

'Can you think of anyone who would want to harm Mr Vitek?' Peiperová enquired.

'No, but whoever it is must be quite old and able to keep a grudge. He's been retired quite a while.'

The detectives rose to leave when a final question occurred to Jerneková. 'I don't suppose you remember the girl's name?'

Helena Borská furrowed her brow and thought hard. 'Gabriela. I can't remember the rest.'

'Never mind. It's a start,' said Peiperová.

'It would be good to know what happened to her and her baby, if you can find her. For my peace of mind, you understand.'

'I'll see if we can trace her.'

Helena's face suddenly lit up. 'I can tell you one thing. She said that the week after she saw me she'd be sixteen and she didn't know if that made a difference to her complaint. So that would be the third week of September. And she must have been born in 1969, because this would have been in 1985.'

As they left, the detectives were unusually silent until Jerneková broke the spell. 'We've got to find her, boss. I want to know she's okay now.'

'Me too.'

CHAPTER 13

Mucha glanced up at the trio marching towards him. 'Coming gang-handed now, are we? It won't work. I'm still retiring.'

'We want to use your exceptional database talents,' said Peiperová.

'Do you now? What exceptional talents are those?'

'We've got three bits of information and we're hoping you can think of a way to link them together to find the information we really want,' Navrátil explained.

'Which is?'

'Where someone is now so we can go and interview her,' Jerneková added.

'What have you got then?'

'She was a fifteen-year-old girl who accused a Politburo member of getting her pregnant,' Navrátil said. 'The StB came to take her to a psychiatric clinic of some kind. Now, their report doesn't give her name — she's only referred to as "the subject" — nor does it give an exact address. But she seems to have lived somewhere in Žižkov.'

'That's useful,' said Mucha. 'That narrows it down to around seventy thousand people.'

'But we've got more,' said Jerneková. 'Her first name is Gabriela, and she was born in the third week of September 1969.'

Mucha wrote the relevant facts on a slip of paper. 'Third week is a bit tricky, because it all depends how you count a week. We might mean full week, or the third week with any September days in it. But if you're sure of the name we can look for females called Gabriela born in September 1969 in the present national ID database.'

'I thought of that,' Navrátil told him. 'There don't appear to be any.'

'If she's still in the psychiatric clinic she may not have needed an ID. But let's try an alternative. She must have had an ID at some time, since she was over fifteen. And if she was sixteen in 1985, she must have been fifteen in 1984.'

'Wow! That's amazing!' said Jerneková, somehow keeping a straight face.

'Any more sarcasm and you're on your own,' warned Mucha. 'The thing is, there are records of every ID card issued, so we may be able to find one newly issued in September 1984 to a girl called Gabriela.' He clicked a few times on his keyboard and waited for the screen to populate. 'Not a thing.'

There was a gentle cough from behind them. A young officer in an impeccable uniform was trying to attract Mucha's attention.

'What is it, Fintr?'

'It's just that, well, I think…'

'Out with it, Fintr. What have I overlooked?'

'Sergeant, the law requires everyone over fifteen to have an ID card. But that doesn't mean you have to be fifteen to have one. She could have been issued with one earlier if she had made a request.'

Mucha nodded approvingly. 'Quite right. See, folks, you won't miss me at all. Fintr can do everything you want.'

'If she lived in Žižkov, she probably got it at the Prague 3 district office,' Fintr added.

'You can get your ID anywhere,' Jerneková pointed out.

'You can, but why stray far from home?' Fintr suggested.

'Especially if you live in Žižkov,' Mucha agreed. 'They're a funny lot there. Let's give it a try. All IDs issued to anyone called Gabriela through the Prague 3 office after September 1969 up to September 1985.'

The computer digested the information and the cursor blinked rhythmically as if to confirm that it was still doing something.

'If it isn't finished by six o'clock I'm going home anyway,' said Jerneková.

'Give it a chance, Lucie,' Peiperová remarked. 'It's churning through millions of records.'

Suddenly the screen began to fill. First three names, appeared, then, after a pause, another two.

'Is that it?' asked Navrátil.

'The cursor is still flashing,' Fintr noted.

Another four names were presented, and by the time the cursor finally disappeared and the words SEARCH COMPLETE appeared on the screen they had seventy-two to look at, spread over two screens.

'I'll print this out,' Mucha announced. He laid two sheets of paper in front of them, and Navrátil ran his finger down the lists.

'There you are!' he said. 'Stašková, Gabriela, born 19 September 1969. And we've got an address.'

'Issued when she was twelve,' Mucha observed. 'I wonder what she did to get that?'

Peiperová offered an answer. 'She was a champion gymnast. Maybe she travelled to take part in competitions.'

'That's plausible,' agreed Mucha. 'Back then you could often use it as a passport within the Eastern Bloc.'

'But why didn't anyone notice she'd stopped competing?' Jerneková wondered.

'We don't know that they didn't. But, anyway, in those days if somebody vanished you didn't want to appear too inquisitive, especially if someone had seen the StB turn up,' Mucha explained. 'And believe me, when the StB arrested people they wanted the neighbours to know about it.'

'But that ID would only have been valid for five years,' Navrátil observed. 'Why haven't we got any sign of it being renewed? Did she die?'

Mucha shook his head sadly. 'Worse than that. By the time she was seventeen she was in a psychiatric clinic, and inmates who are deemed not to have capacity to make their own decisions don't get ID. She might be dead, but she might also still be in the clinic.'

Slonský shuddered. A cold shiver ran up his spine. He downed the remains of his drink and got off his chair, ready to move to a table away from the window. He rubbed his eyes, just to check that he was not hallucinating. He was not. That really was Major Klinger sitting waiting for a train.

Things got worse. The next time he looked Grigar was there too. It was then that the full horror of his situation seized him. They must be going to Bratislava too. For all Klinger's foibles, he was an excellent fraud officer, though who was minding the shop when the more senior fifty per cent of the manpower was on a jolly to Slovakia was an interesting question.

The departure board shone mockingly as it reminded him that the train journey to Bratislava would take four hours and twenty-three minutes; and that was a minimum. If it did not run to time, it could be even longer. He wouldn't mind betting that they had been allocated adjoining seats too, though he supposed that he did not have to sit in one of them. He could find another place elsewhere in the train. Somewhere near the buffet, he fancied. Even at the buffet counter, if there were stools.

Sadly, his failure to move during this reverie meant that Grigar spotted him. Worse yet, he was walking over to talk to him. There were a great many people in Prague whom Slonský did not like, a considerable number of them being police officers, and Grigar was quite close to the top of the list.

'Are you going to Bratislava too?' Grigar asked.

'Yes, I am,' said Slonský. 'Are you still organising crime?'

'Head of the Organised Crime Squad, to be more precise.'

'That's what I said,' Slonský insisted.

'Hardly. Are you still murdering people?'

Just about to start, thought Slonský, but then decided not to aggravate a fellow traveller so early in the journey. 'I leave that to criminals,' he said. 'Then I catch them.'

His orders had insisted that those attending should wear their best uniform. Slonský had done so, grateful that he had been issued a new jacket when he was promoted, because he could no longer button up his old one.

'Still a captain?' Grigar asked, pointing at Slonský's shoulders.

'Yes. You?'

'Just got my major's chevron and star.'

'Ah. I thought you might have borrowed a uniform.'

'Rajka not coming, then?'

'No. Urgent business of an unspecified nature.'

'I wish I'd thought of that,' Grigar sighed. 'Drink?'

Slonský did not recall the last time Grigar had offered him a drink. 'Well, just to be sociable,' he replied.

'You? Sociable? That'll be the day.'

'Is that Major Klinger? Should we invite him to join us?'

Grigar had been speaking to Klinger just a few minutes before, but he still turned round to check before answering.

'No point. What do you think the chances are that he'll accept a drink in a glass someone else has used?' he said.

'I've seen him drink a glass of white wine in a restaurant once.'

'He didn't strain it through his hankie first?'

'No. Just gritted his teeth and sipped it till it was all gone.'

'God Almighty, I wish I'd seen that.'

'What happens at these meetings, then?'

'Have you read the papers?'

Slonský debated whether to say yes (and risk being found out) or no (and be thought unprepared). 'I've skimmed them,' he answered. 'I only got them yesterday.'

'Well, you didn't need to. They'll read them out loud all over again. Then we ask questions for clarification, then we all say what a wonderful paper it was and how well things are going, and then it'll be the turn for the other country to read one of their papers.'

'So I'll have to read the criminal police report?'

'Maybe, maybe not. We stop at four o'clock and take the remaining papers as read. Did you bring any lunch?'

'I thought they fed us?'

'They do, but, you know, Slovak cooking.'

'Such as?'

'Sheep cheese soup. Sheep cheese dumplings. Do you detect a theme?'

'I might have a big breakfast,' Slonský said.

'Good idea.'

Slonský had not remembered to take a book. In fact, the idea had never crossed his mind. It was quite a while since he had endured a long train journey and he had no idea how he would occupy his time. This problem was exacerbated by the absence of anywhere to sit near the buffet. The train had an "at seat trolley service", but unfortunately the woman with the trolley could not be persuaded to wait by Slonský's seat and he was forced to wait until it came back.

Klinger was no company at all. He was keeping up his German by reading a volume of poetry. In an attempt to make polite conversation Slonský had suggested that Klinger should translate one of the poems and read it out.

'That's not much of a poem,' he protested.

'Well, obviously in German it has a consistent rhythm that the Czech translation doesn't have,' Klinger argued.

'I only know one poem,' Slonský mused, and recited a comic verse he had learned as a child that made Grigar's eyebrows shoot up while he checked no nearby passengers were offended by its scatological tone.

'It's not exactly Heine, is it?' Klinger remarked drily before returning to his book, leaving Slonský to turn to Grigar for entertainment.

'Arrested anyone interesting lately?' he asked.

Slonský was bored with listening to Grigar recounting his team's latest triumphs. He wanted to monopolise the conversation for a while with his favourite collars, but then it occurred to him that Grigar might be able to help him.

'Did you know Dominik Vitek?' Slonský asked.

'Vitek? I can't say I knew him, but he was mentioned once or twice. I saw in the newspaper that he'd died.'

'Died? That's one way of putting it. Clubbed to death with one of those French cast-iron frying pans. Is there any connection with organised crime?'

Grigar was too old a hand to give a definite answer. 'Not that I'm aware of. Why do you ask?'

'We found a lot of files in Vitek's safe. I'd have put good money on them being blackmail material given what is in them, except that Vitek doesn't seem to have made any money from them.'

'Maybe he had a bank account you don't know about.'

'Unlikely,' Klinger chipped in. 'Unless it's in another name, like a company or a charity. But even then he has to take the money out sometime, and banks are very suspicious of people withdrawing substantial amounts of cash from company accounts. And he's not in the register of company directors or charitable trustees.'

'Could it be abroad?' Grigar asked.

'Same issue,' Klinger insisted. 'There's no point unless he brings the money back, and he'd have to get it out of the country in the first place. Is there any evidence of repeated trips abroad?'

'I don't think so,' Slonský answered, 'but I'll have to get Navrátil to check.'

'I thought it was Navrátil's case?' Klinger commented.

'So it is,' Slonský agreed. 'I meant that I'll suggest that he checks it.'

'Maybe if you can't find a motive, you're looking in the wrong place,' Grigar claimed.

'Meaning?'

Grigar smiled. 'I remember a case a few years back with a car parts supplier. They were convinced one of their employees was up to something, but every time he was stopped at the gates he had documentation for everything on his fork-lift truck.'

'Was he forging the documentation?' Klinger asked.

'No, he was stealing fork-lift trucks. By the time he was stopped there were eight missing.'

*

Krob was feeling a little left out of things, so when Navrátil returned to the office with the address in Žižkov he jumped at the opportunity to go with Navrátil on the off-chance that one of Gabriela's family still lived there.

'After all,' Navrátil said, 'if she was born in September 1969, Gabriela would be thirty-nine now, so there's a good chance her mother is still alive.'

Krob clicked a few keys. 'There's nobody called Stašková at that address now.'

'Maybe not. But if your daughter has been arrested or you've got divorced you might go under another name. Anyway, there may be someone who can tell us where they've gone.'

Krob tapped his teeth was his pencil. It was a habit when he was thinking. 'If she had a child in early 1986, they would be around twenty-three now. Easily old enough to be a suspect themselves.'

'From what I've heard it's likely she had a forced abortion, but it's another thing we ought to check. Make a note of it for the file so we don't forget.'

Navrátil sighed. 'We're collecting red herrings,' he said, 'but I'm not sure which they are. So many things to follow up, and we know most of them will be a waste of time.'

'Isn't that always the case?' Krob replied.

'I suppose so. But sometimes you get one lead that jumps out as the obvious one to follow first, and I'm not feeling that here.'

'Let's follow this one, and then we can have a recap with the whole team,' Krob suggested.

'It won't be the whole team. Captain Slonský isn't here.'

'Agreed, but he's been pretty hands-off on this one. Anyway, when you next report to him, a recapitulation of what we've learned will be a help to you.'

Navrátil lifted his jacket from the back of his chair and slipped it on. 'As usual, you're correct. We'll do this and then I'll bring our notes right up to date. We may as well use the Metro.'

As Krob had feared, the family now living at Gabriela Stašková's old home knew nothing about it.

'That's it, then,' shrugged Navrátil. 'We've hit a dead end.'

'Maybe,' Krob answered, 'but I've got an idea.' He pointed across the road to a second floor flat where an old woman was sitting by the window. Together they dodged the traffic and climbed the stairs. Krob knocked on the door which was opened after a while by a young girl who had to stand on tiptoe to reach the handle. 'Is that your grandma by the window?' he asked.

'My great-grandma,' said the girl.

'We're from the police,' Krob continued. 'Could we come in and talk to her?'

'I'm not allowed to let people in,' she said, 'in case they're burglars.'

'That's quite right. How about if you take my ID to show great-grandma and ask her if we can come in?'

After due consideration the girl agreed, and promptly slammed the door in their faces.

'What are you going to do if she doesn't come back?' asked Navrátil. 'Losing a police ID may pose a few problems for you.'

'I'd have to kick the door in,' Krob replied.

'And your legal basis for doing that is…?'

'That I believe a crime is in the process of being committed.'

'What crime?'

'Theft of an ID card. Section 205, sub-section 1 of the Criminal Code.'

The door opened again and the girl solemnly handed the card to Krob. 'Great-grandma says you can come in,' she announced.

They passed through a dark hallway into a sitting room where the old woman was sitting by the window peeling potatoes.

Navrátil and Krob introduced themselves.

'Your little one is very sensible,' Krob said.

'Not bad for her age. My granddaughter leaves her with me while she's at work. It's company.'

'Tiring, though,' said Krob. 'I've got a son of the same age. He never stops.'

'I don't know where she gets the energy. She wears me out just watching her.'

'We're sorry to trouble you, but I'm hoping you might be able to help us. Have you lived here long?'

'Since 1954. These flats weren't long built when my husband and I moved in.'

'That's what I was hoping. We're trying to find out what happened to a family who lived opposite. I wonder if you knew them. There was a teenaged girl called Gabriela Stašková and I guess her parents lived there too.'

'Gabriela? Yes, I remember her.'

'What can you tell us about her?' asked Navrátil.

'She was a nice girl. We didn't spend a lot of time with her, but there was a good community spirit back then. People were in and out of each other's apartments all day long. I looked after her once or twice when her mother had to be somewhere. Her father was no use, you see. She worked nights and he was supposed to get back from the pub before she went out. Complete waste of space, he was. I only really knew Gabriela and her mother, Jitka. It was terrible, what happened to them.'

'Can you tell us anything about that?' Krob asked.

'I'm not one to gossip,' the old woman began.

Krob knew enough about old women to know that he was expected to say 'Perish the thought!' or something similar, so he did.

'Gabriela was quite a gymnast,' the woman continued. 'She was tall for her age and naturally graceful, and it seemed almost every week she was coming back with a cup or a medal. Anyway, she met a man, and he paid her a bit of attention and her head was turned. I don't need to tell you that when a young girl gets in trouble like that, she's usually led on by the man. She was beside herself, and her poor mother likewise. The man wanted nothing to do with her and wouldn't meet his responsibilities.

'But then Jitka found out he was married, and she was desperate. She thought if she could talk to the wife, woman to woman, so to speak, she might get some sympathy. At the very least she'd make his life hard for him. But before she got there Gabriela beat her to it. From what I could make out, the wife was shocked, but she didn't deny it. She gave Gabriela a bit of money, not to buy her off, but to try to make things a little better for her. Anyway, a few days after that we see a car waiting in the street. There weren't that many cars around here then. Gabriela comes down the road and these two men bundle her into the car and drive off. Next thing we hear she's in the asylum.'

'Asylum?' Navrátil interrupted.

'They said she was having hysterical delusions. Jitka was allowed to visit a couple of times, but then she takes it into her head to visit the wife too, to see if she can help. The woman wouldn't let her in, said she couldn't do anything. And the next time Jitka visits, Gabriela's been moved to an asylum in the country somewhere and they won't tell her where.' The old woman pulled a tissue from her apron pocket and dabbed her eyes. 'That was the last straw for Jitka.'

'Do you know what happened to her?' Navrátil asked.

'Gassed herself, didn't she? Don't say anything to the folks there now. I'd hate to think I was cooking my dinner in the very room where some poor soul ended it all.'

'And her father?' Krob prompted.

'Hit the bottle. Hard, if you know what I mean.'

'Is he dead too?'

'Didn't live more than eighteen months after his wife died.'

'I don't suppose you ever heard where Gabriela went?'

'It's funny you should mention that. One day, about fifteen years ago, a man turned up right out of the blue looking for Jitka and her husband. He knew they had lived here, you see, but he didn't seem to know they'd died. He said he worked for some government agency and he was trying to find them to put them in touch with their daughter. I told him they were both dead, so he asked if there were any other relatives. I said I didn't know of any. I told him I'd known Gabriela and asked how she was. He said she was physically all right, but being in that place hadn't done much for her mental state. He said seeing as I wasn't family he couldn't tell me any details, not without checking with Gabriela's carers first. All he could tell me was that she had been as far away as the authorities could have sent her, almost in Hungary.'

Navrátil thanked the old lady for her help. The detectives were about to leave when she called them back.

'If you find Gabriela, you will let me know, won't you?'

CHAPTER 14

'This case gets more and more depressing,' Peiperová said.

'They really put women in mental hospitals for getting pregnant?' Jerneková queried.

'So it appears,' Navrátil replied. 'We've only got her word for it, but it fits with stuff the boss has told us in the past.'

'Maybe Mucha can help us find out what happened to Gabriela,' Krob added.

They trooped downstairs to find a suspicious desk sergeant gazing balefully at them.

'Whatever you've dreamed up, the answer is still no,' Mucha said.

'We hoped you can give us a steer with our enquiry,' Navrátil began, and described the interview that he and Krob had conducted earlier in Žižkov.

'Želiezovce,' said Mucha.

'Come again?' Jerneková answered.

'Želiezovce. A labour camp in Slovakia. It's so far east it's almost in Hungary. It was a sort of secure farm. Plenty of women were sent there in the past to pick stuff. The great plus of it was that even if people escaped it was in the middle of nowhere. They couldn't get across the border so the guards would know which way they'd gone, and it's a heck of a walk back to Prague.'

'You think they sent her there?' Navrátil enquired.

'It's only a guess,' said Mucha, 'but it's the best suggestion I've got. And I can guess who the guy was who went looking for her family. Let's assume that by the time the Communists fall from power she's become institutionalized. Maybe it happened before then. Even if they know she shouldn't be there, they can't just throw her out to fend for herself. But in 1993 the Czechs and Slovaks divorce and the country is divided. The Slovaks don't want Czechs in their prisons and camps, so there was a big swap. But with folks who were in detention for reasons other than a prison sentence, the Ministry would try to find somewhere suitable for them. They'd see if their families could take them back.'

'Thinking about it,' said Krob, 'he told the old lady that "she had been" far away, not that she *was* far away.'

'There you are, then,' said Mucha. 'She was still alive fifteen years ago, and if they couldn't place her with her family, she'll have gone into state psychiatric care. You could ask the Ministry if they have her somewhere.'

'I hate to appear cruel,' said Navrátil, 'but if we can't see how she can be connected to our case we ought to hand it on to someone else to look into.'

'You're right,' said Jerneková. 'You don't want to appear cruel.'

'Lucie,' Peiperová rebuked her, 'it's Jan's investigation. And it wouldn't be a productive use of our time.'

'Neither is beer and sausage,' said Jerneková, 'but that doesn't seem to stop the boss. It's one question, that's all. Do they know where she is, or not?'

Navrátil raised his hands in surrender. 'Okay. You can make the call. Let's see if we can make some sort of progress in this case.'

Like Slonský, Navrátil believed in the occasional team meeting to pick through all the evidence collected so far in a case. Unlike Slonský, he did not hold it in a bar or café, but in the office that Peiperová shared with Jerneková so that the men would bring their chairs two doors along the corridor.

'We don't have any additional forensic information,' Navrátil began. 'The pan was the murder weapon but there were no usable prints. The folders in the safe have given us a number of names, but some are untraceable thus far, or are such common names that we cannot be sure that we have the right person. Despite this we have been able to find and interview a number of women. Let's take each in turn.'

'Renáta Orenková,' said Peiperová. 'Husband was Viktor Skála. He went to prison for some time but we haven't been able to trace if he's out and about yet. There are strong suspicions that Vitek put him there.'

'The odds are that Skála has died,' Krob added, 'because he isn't in prison and we can't find a current ID in that name. But there is the possibility that he has changed his name.'

'Even then, the ID register should note that,' Navrátil responded, before conceding, 'but of course we know such events sometimes slip through. Who's next?'

'Věra Slonská, I suppose,' said Krob.

'I think that's a red herring,' Navrátil opined.

'I thought the boss said that the StB wouldn't put something in the files unless they believed there was a link,' Jerneková interrupted.

'When did he say that? He doesn't know about Věra's involvement and it's best kept that way for now.'

'He said it about another case, but the principle holds true.'

Navrátil shrugged. 'She says she can't think of a link and I believe her. Unless we've got something positive to put to her, I think we have to move on or we'll waste time going up blind alleys.'

'Lenka Lipská,' said Jerneková. 'Quite a sweet old lady, but still living in the Sixties.'

'She seemed genuinely upset that Vitek was dead and if she already knew that, then she's a very good actress,' said Krob.

'But that's exactly what she is,' Peiperová observed. 'A professional actress. It would be a sad day if she couldn't feign that. Maria Suková definitely had reason to remember Vitek, but if her story is true then she had every reason to be grateful to him. And she wants to know when his body is released for a funeral, by the way.'

'She'd say that if she killed him, though, wouldn't she?' Jerneková slipped in. 'Didn't I read somewhere that murderers often like to go to their victim's funerals?'

'So do a lot of people who aren't murderers, Lucie,' Krob told her. 'You wouldn't get an arrest warrant based on that.'

'Then Jakub Petrák mentioned Ditka Hrubešová, who had a baby who was adopted. We ought to chase that lead up when we've got a moment,' Navrátil said. 'After all, if the baby blames Vitek for being adopted, they might have a grudge against him.' He checked his notebook again. 'Petrák also told us about Zdenka Pálková. She was a florist the council tried to bully off her pitch by the cemetery. We could dig into that a bit further. But my money is on Anežka Morusová.'

'Didn't you say she was dead?' Peiperová interjected.

'Well, yes…'

'I'd have said that was a pretty good alibi.'

'But before that she had published a story accusing a Politburo member, Vladimir Borský, of getting an underage girl pregnant.'

'Bastard,' Jerneková said. 'And I'm not going to apologise for saying it this time.'

'Borský is dead too,' Navrátil continued.

'It probably wasn't him, then,' Jerneková concluded, 'but he's still a bastard.'

'If I may continue,' Navrátil remarked with a sideways look at Jerneková, 'we know that Morusová got the story from Borský's wife, Helena Borská. And we've found out that the girl's name was Gabriela AAašková. She had ample reason for hating Borský, who had her committed to a mental institution, but no obvious reason for hating Vitek, who was only obliquely connected to the whole thing because Borská told Morusová the story in The Ladies' Lounge that he ran.'

'Don't forget we haven't yet found out what happened to Gabriela's baby, who would now be in their early twenties,' Krob reminded him.

'True. But why would that child even know of the existence of Vitek?'

'Maybe they got a garbled version of the story and thought that Vitek was the one who got their mum pregnant?' Jerneková suggested.

There was a long silence before Navrátil summed up. 'So that's where we are. I'll bring the case notes up to date before I brief Colonel Rajka tomorrow. In the meantime, if you can think of something useful to do, please do it.'

You had to hand it to Mucha, thought Navrátil, he had played a blinder that afternoon. The file on Viktor Skála had been found, revealing that he had indeed been sentenced to eight years' imprisonment in 1979, of which he had served nearly ten when the Berlin Wall came down, his parole hearing having revealed that he had been too generously treated by the trial judge given his heinous crimes. Skála was released at the end of 1989 and went to live in a hostel, but a few months later he was arrested because he had made a scene at a former colleague's house while asking for help. He was released with a warning but evicted from the hostel, and was subsequently detained twice for begging and vagrancy. He died in 1992, which made it very unlikely that he or anyone closely connected to him might have played any part in Vitek's death.

The greater triumph, in Navrátil's view, was that Mucha had found a lead on Gabriela Stašková. In 1993 she had been transferred from her labour camp in Želiezovce to a prison in Opava which had a psychiatric assessment unit. While he could not find any evidence that she was still there, he had discovered that she had been temporarily in the care of the psychiatric hospital in Opava. She was no longer there either, but the good news was that she had been sent for care in a convent. The convent did not appear to have a telephone, but Mucha had asked the local police to verify where she now was and was expecting an answer in the next twenty-four hours. The psychiatric hospital had still been seeing Gabriela as late as 2004, and while there was no doubt that she had been severely damaged by her forced incarceration, they had been hopeful that she would eventually be able to live semi-independently. The bad news was that she had suffered a forced abortion and had, indeed, been sterilised at the age of sixteen as a "moral degenerate".

Navrátil walked through to the women's office with Mucha's note and handed it to Peiperová without a word. She in turn gave it to Jerneková.

'I take it back,' said Jerneková. 'I thought Borský was a bastard, and now I know that doesn't do him justice. This God of yours,' she said to Navrátil, 'is he going to punish Borský like he deserves?'

'It depends whether he repented,' Navrátil replied. 'Like it or not, if I want my sins forgiven I have to accept that the same rules apply to others.'

'You haven't got any sins,' argued Jerneková.

'Believe me, I have.'

'Leaving the top off the mayonnaise jar doesn't count,' Jerneková told him. 'Anyway, Borský died suddenly, so let's hope he never got round to asking for forgiveness. And if I catch you sneaking into a church to do it for him, I won't be responsible for my actions.'

It was as well that Slonský had arrived in the breakfast room of the hotel promptly at seven o'clock, because he was still there at half past eight, attacking the buffet with all the gusto and application of a brown bear anticipating the coming of winter.

'The car will be here in fifteen minutes,' Grigar reminded him, 'and don't forget we're not coming back, so bring your luggage.'

'I have,' said Slonský, holding up a plastic shopping bag with his laundry and toilet kit in it.

By mid-morning he was wondering when they were going to have a break. The plate of biscuits in front of him was empty and he could have killed for a coffee. It was affecting his concentration, because he had not been able to make any sense of his Slovak counterpart's presentation.

A bored Slonský is a terrible thing. He had just thought of a particularly fiendish question to ask his opposite number when the chairman said that after the questions there would be a twenty-minute coffee break, so Slonský decided that his question was not that urgent.

'After the interval Captain Slonský will give his presentation,' the chairman continued.

This gave Slonský around twenty minutes to write one, since he had assumed that the document Rajka had given him spoke for itself. He chomped on a pastry while he re-read it, and when they reconvened he straightened his tie, smiled benignly at the assembly, and began to speak.

'Colonel Rajka sends his apologies for not being able to attend himself. I'll do you all the compliment of assuming that you have read his paper. It seems to me to be self-explanatory, so I suggest that we go straight to any questions and save valuable time for other matters.'

As he had expected, some of those present had not read the paper but did not want to admit the fact, so there were no questions. Slonský thanked them for their attention and resumed his seat.

The attendees had been allocated an hour for lunch, which was a sit-down affair. Serving dishes were passed up and down the table, but most came to rest close to Slonský. The drinks offered were varieties of mineral water, something which had not passed Slonský's lips for some time (and he wasn't going to start now) and he was about to complain that the sausages were past their best before date when someone pointed out that they were a vegan substitute. After that he checked each dish carefully to ensure that the cabbage really was cabbage, the onions were not fried flower bulbs and the pastry was not cardboard. The chef had sprinkled something chopped and green over the mashed potato, so Slonský turned it over with the serving spoon to take a portion from the lower depths.

Once, a long time ago, Mucha had demonstrated that it was possible to set your mobile phone to ring as if you were receiving a call. You could then apologise profusely that urgent business had called you away, even though it was only the alarm clock function sounding. Unfortunately, Slonský could not remember how it was done, and caused some consternation by accidentally triggering the news headlines at full volume as he tried various buttons at random. Eventually he settled down, soothed in some measure by Grigar's whispered remark that, by common consent, nobody asked any questions about anything after lunch in the hope that they might finish early. Sadly this convention had eluded Klinger, who asked a string of technical questions about international money laundering. It took Slonský a while to realise that this involved more than accidentally leaving a hundred-crown note in your shirt when you washed it. This in turn caused him to wonder where he had left his train ticket, so he searched each pocket in turn until he remembered that it was in his wallet.

Eventually the meeting drew to a close, and Slonský was pleased when Grigar apologised to their hosts that they must dash if they were to catch the next train back. The considerate Slovaks had arranged a fleet of police cars with sirens and flashing lights to take the Czechs to the railway station, which was done so expeditiously that Slonský had time to purchase a couple of baguettes before the train departed.

Klinger occupied himself in annotating a document, for which purpose he produced an array of highlighter pens from his briefcase. Grigar dropped his head back and closed his eyes in anticipation of sleep. It was at this point that Slonský remembered that he had left his plastic bag of dirty laundry, toothbrush and razor on the counter at the station snack bar in Bratislava.

The train rolled into the main station in Prague a little after half-past eight, and a few minutes later Slonský alighted from the Metro near police headquarters. His inclination was to leave a note saying in the light of his long day he would be in late the next morning, but he thought he ought first to check that he had not missed anything. The fact that he had nothing better to do with his evenings and often worked late led to his assumption that others would do the same, so he was a little surprised when, after a short detour to buy a new razor and toothbrush, he found Sergeant Salzer on the front desk and nobody in his team's offices. He still had the folder of papers from his meeting under his arm, which he dropped on his desk to avoid having to take them home, and looked in on the women's office first. Peiperová, who could file in her sleep, had an empty desk. Jerneková's bore half a jar of pickles, one badly knitted sock, and a selection of pencils with heavily chewed ends.

The men's office was rather different. Slonský's old desk, which he still used in preference to that in his own office, was a mess, as if the Czech Republic had entered a "How much can you get on a standard desk?" competition. Krob's was neat, but bore several sticky notes reminding him of things to do in the morning. These carried cryptic commands such as "Chase Opava in the morning", "Check Ms Orenková knows about Borský" and "Book in for child vaccinations".

Navrátil's was impeccable, with a neat folder sitting right in the middle of the blotter. It was labelled "Vitek Enquiry" and the top document was a report on progress so far that Navrátil had signed and dated that day. Being Navrátil, it had been timed at 16:48, just in case something important had taken place at 16:50 which he might have been accused of overlooking. Having nothing better to do, Slonský settled down to read it, and was congratulating himself, quite unjustly, on having taught Navrátil to write good reports, when he came upon a name he knew.

Jolted upright, Slonský read that Věra had not been able to suggest any reason why the StB had her name in its files and had denied any connection to Dominik Vitek. Her new address was noted there, which Slonský copied down before lobbing the folder back on Navrátil's desk and storming out of the office door.

It was a measure of the importance that Slonský attached to this information that he hailed a taxi and was soon hammering on the grubby door of a small flat in the south of town.

'What do you want at this time of night?' his estranged wife demanded when she opened the door, and if she was less than gracious in her greeting, that was nothing compared with Slonský's demeanour.

'Are you going to let me in, or do we have a conversation on your doorstep?' he asked.

'If you don't lower your voice it won't matter whether you're inside or out.'

'I want a word with you.'

'Well, I don't want a word with you,' she replied with spirit, attempting to close the door. Slonský quickly jammed his foot over the threshold and yelped as the door slammed into his big toe.

'This is official business,' he growled.

Věra stepped back to allow him in. 'Are you going to caution me first?' she asked.

'Been through this before, have you? Probably picked up by the Vice Squad once or twice.'

Věra slapped him across the cheek.

'That's assaulting a police officer,' he said.

'I'm assaulting my husband who happens to be a rude moron,' she responded.

'You haven't shown me any identification proving you're a police officer.'

'You know I've been one for over forty years.'

'I know what else you've been for over forty years, but I'm not saying it in case you arrest me.'

'Dominik Vitek,' Slonský hissed. 'Why did the StB link you to him?'

'I told Navrátil I didn't have any idea. Aren't you two on speaking terms?'

'Apparently not, because he hasn't told me, his superior, that he'd been to interview you. I'll deal with him in due course. You're the one I'm questioning now.'

'And I'm the one saying I don't know this Vitek character, and that should be good enough for you.'

'Then why did the StB think you did?'

'I don't know, do I? You used to say yourself they were a useless bunch of incompetents. Maybe that's your answer.'

'Why would they make something like this up?'

'Think of all the times they stitched people up in the past.'

'Why would they bother to make something up about you?'

'Maybe it's not about me. Maybe it's to do with this Vibek…'

'Vitek. Dominik Vitek.'

'Vitek, then. I don't know him. I have no idea why the StB thought I did.'

'If you know something it's your duty to tell me.'

'If I knew something I wouldn't need you to tell me my duty. Now, I want to go to bed, so either arrest me or get lost.'

'Don't tempt me. You needn't think being married to me would protect you.'

'I've never thought being married to you was to my advantage before, so why should I think that now?' Věra held the door open and gestured to Slonský to go through it. 'Nice to see you again, Josef. Now go to hell.'

CHAPTER 15

Navrátil was bemused. The folder that he had left neatly in the centre of his blotter was now carelessly tossed to one side. When he opened it and saw the thumb marks where one sheet had been tightly gripped, he had a fairly good idea who had been reading it, and he was equally sure that his cunning plan to keep the information from his boss for as long as possible had failed; but, just in case it had not, he did not feel that he could say anything.

In any case, he could not say anything until Slonský arrived for work, but equally he did not feel able to take the folder to Colonel Rajka without letting Slonský, his immediate superior, know he was doing so, unless, of course, Rajka specifically asked for it. It was all rather vexing.

The door was eventually flung back and Slonský marched in. Without bothering to remove his hat or coat he pointed an accusing finger at Navrátil. 'I want a word with you!'

Navrátil braced himself for a verbal onslaught, but it did not come, because immediately behind Slonský came Mucha, whose brows appeared blacker and thicker than usual.

'And I want a word with *you*! Gentlemen, this would be a good time for you to get and a coffee.'

Krob and Navrátil needed no further invitation, but Slonský interrupted.

'I'm their boss, and I decide when they have coffee.'

'Make the most of it because you won't be their boss for much longer if you don't listen to me,' Mucha bellowed back.

The unusual vehemence of Mucha's words took Slonský by surprise, and he offered no resistance to the two detectives sneaking past him. Navrátil had taken the precaution of tucking the folder under his arm, having decided that this would be a very good time to take it to Rajka before Slonský ordered him to alter it. Mucha ushered them out and shut the door.

'What the hell were you playing at?'

'Come again?'

'What was going through your tiny pea-sized brain that made you think it was all right to go to Věra's flat and bully her?'

'Has she been whingeing to you?'

'She telephoned the station to complain and luckily for you I took the call. She is furious, and I can't say I blame her.'

'She's a material witness in a murder enquiry and she's withholding information.'

Mucha prodded Slonský in the chest. 'Even if that was true, you know the rules about interviewing family and friends. You know you should have got someone else to go, like Navrátil.'

'He'd already been and he got nowhere with her. He doesn't know her like I do.'

'That's just the point. You know her. You shouldn't have been within a kilometre of her door. By rights I should tell Colonel Rajka and he'd send it to Major Lukas for a professional standards enquiry. All that holds me back is the knowledge that if I do that your chances of getting your contract extended at the end of the year will be nil. Didn't that cross your mind?'

Having passed the age of fifty-nine, Slonský was now on a one-year contract, renewable only at his boss's pleasure each birthday. The thought of retirement made him gulp involuntarily. It was the one thing that really scared him; that, and Dumpy Anna in the canteen refusing to serve him when he forgot his wallet.

The door opened and the considerable muscle and crisp light blue shirt of Colonel Rajka entered the room.

'Sergeant Mucha? What are you doing here? Would you mind giving us a few minutes for a private discussion?'

'Of course, sir,' said Mucha, pointing at Slonský as he left and adding, 'I'll be back to finish this later.'

As the door closed behind him, Rajka took a deep breath that seemed to puff up his chest like a giant bullfrog. 'Is that about what I want to talk to you about, or have you done two incredibly stupid and improper things?' Rajka asked.

'Sir?'

'Don't play the innocent with me, Captain. Your career is hanging by a thread. You would do well to show some contrition.'

'It's not how it looks, sir.'

'It had better not be. I've just spoken to Officer Fintr. Let me tell you how it looks to me. A woman who lives alone and is peripherally attached to a live investigation, about which she has already been questioned by the lead investigating officer personally, whose judgement was that she had no useful information to offer, has nevertheless been harangued late at night by a close family member in an aggressive, perhaps even threatening way. Is that a fair summary, Slonský?'

Slonský pouted his lower lip a little. 'I'm not a close family member. I was just married to her, that's all.'

'You still are, in the eyes of the law.'

'We've been separated for thirty-eight years.'

'But not divorced. And frankly, married, separated or divorced, there is a conflict of interest here that should have jumped out like a stampeding rhino even through your thick skull.'

Slonský decided it was time to go on the offensive. 'I'm Navrátil's superior, and if I think that he hasn't investigated a lead properly it's my duty to follow it up myself.'

'No, it's your duty to ensure that it is properly followed up by a competent officer who doesn't have a conflict of interest. Let me lay this out very clearly for you. If Mrs Slonská persists in her complaint then I will have no choice but to pass it to Major Lukas, and he will have no choice but to suspend you while he investigates. From what I can see of your past joint history, he has already done you enough favours for two lifetimes. You can't expect any more.'

Slonský could see it was unlikely that he would win this argument. 'What do you suggest I do, sir?'

'I suggest you do nothing. You will not go within a hundred metres of your wife. I'm going to visit her to apologise on the department's behalf, but I won't influence her decision. Nor will you take it out on Navrátil. He doesn't know that you were actually dim-witted enough to see her, though I suspect that he has now guessed from Mucha's demeanour what has happened. Navrátil was hoping that we could stop you going. He had your back, though God knows you don't deserve it.'

There was a silence while Rajka attempted to compose himself. When he next spoke his voice was quieter. 'Is there the slightest chance that you have any awareness at all of the impropriety of what you have done, or am I talking to the wall?'

Slonský weighed up two possible answers, both of which were variants on the word no, but even he could see that a different response was expected of him. 'I can see that my actions were open to an uncharitable interpretation,' he replied.

Rajka tried a different tack. 'Suppose Peiperová had been kidnapped, and Navrátil appointed himself as the investigating officer, what would you say?'

'It's funny you should mention that, sir, because she was once…'

'It's a hypothetical example, Slonský! What would you say?'

'How can it be hypothetical if it happened?'

'And what did you tell Navrátil?'

Slonský subsided. 'I told him he was too close and to leave it to me.'

'And that was excellent advice. So take it yourself. Now, as for this case, Navrátil will report to me. He can involve you as much or as little as he thinks fit, but whatever happens you do not speak to Mrs Slonská about it again. Is that clear?'

'Yes, sir. What if she rings me to say she's remembered something?'

'You find someone else to take her statement. Me, if necessary. Now, you might want to go and make your peace with Sergeant Mucha, who doesn't seem very pleased with you.'

Rajka left the room, and Slonský thought about going down to the front desk to speak to his old friend, but decided to go to the canteen instead.

Things were rather quiet after that. When Slonský returned he could see no sign of Navrátil and Krob, who had decided that the most profitable use of their time would be to travel five hundred kilometres to Opava and back to see if they could meet Gabriela Stašková, since the police there had left a message to say that they had tracked her down. The idea had then occurred to them that she might prefer to speak to the women officers, but rather than sending them instead, Navrátil had opted for a works outing for all four of them, ostensibly so that they could share the driving, though this invitation was not extended to Jerneková, much to her disgust. With nothing much to do, Slonský had decided that a quarter past ten was near enough to lunchtime to go in search of Valentin, who was likely to be more understanding than anyone else.

Slonský and Valentin had known each other since they started school. They had been drinking together since they were eleven, often up in the treehouse that Valentin's father had built for them. Mr Valentin senior was a carpenter, though the many hours he spent in his shed may have had more to do with the copious supplies of vodka stashed there than any great desire to build things in wood.

Valentin's mother was a nice woman, thought Slonský. Many's the time she had patched up his scuffed knee, sewn a tear in his school trousers or set an extra place at the dinner table for him. He had loved his own parents, of course, but his mother was not hot like Valentin's. In the heat of summer she often had one more blouse button undone than his mother would have dared. It was very curious, Slonský pondered, that a beefy man like Valentin's dad and a definite looker like his mum had produced a scrawny little runt like Valentin. So much for genetics.

This reminiscence led him to recollections of Valentin's sister. She was quite a bit younger than her brother, so when Slonský went away to do his national service in the army she had been a spotty thirteen-year-old with plaits. In his head, she still was. He made a mental note to ask Valentin if he had any recent photographs of her.

He pushed open the door of the third bar that he had tried and spotted a familiar figure writing in longhand on a rather tatty notepad while he sipped a pear brandy. 'When's your deadline?' he asked.

'I'm at the mercy of events,' said Valentin. 'Do I write the story as if the inevitable has happened, or write a holding piece while I wait?'

'What's it about?'

'I've got the headline,' Valentin answered. 'Famous Prague detective kicked off force for malpractice.'

'Have you been talking to Mucha?'

'I came looking for you to give you this fax from my contacts in Slovakia. Mucha said you'd stormed out and when I asked him to give it to you he told me what he would do with it. It's hard enough to read as it is. Shoving it up there won't help with its legibility.'

'You came into the police building?'

'It's a measure of my friendship that I overcame my phobia to deliver it. Mind you, I propped the door open just in case they tried to keep me in.'

'It's good that somebody at least values my friendship.'

'Do I detect that all is not rosy between you and Sergeant Mucha?'

'He tore me off a strip.'

'Why, what did you do?'

'Nothing! Just went to see Věra to see if I could flesh out her statement a bit, that's all.'

'Věra?'

'Yes.'

'As in your wife Věra?'

'Don't rub it in. I try to forget that bit. I didn't let it influence our interview.'

'And I assume that Mucha told you that going on your own to interview a family member who is somehow involved in a murder case was a crass error of judgement?'

'That's his opinion.'

'I think it's fact, Josef.'

'Some friend you are. I come out in search of a loyal companion who will listen to my side of the story and not prejudge my actions, and you turn on me like a quidditch.'

'I think you mean like a quisling. A quidditch is … something to do with Harry Potter.'

'Who?'

'Never mind. Young people stuff. Look, good friends tell you when you've gone wrong. You're not a bad person, but you sometimes make bad choices.'

'Says the man who once tried to go home by Ferris wheel after a night out.'

'I admit my faults. I'd had too much. I know that.'

Slonský chuckled. 'Damn funny though. That moment when you tried to find the machine to stamp your ticket still cracks me up. "It must be at the other end of the tram", you said, and tried to open the door to get out.'

'It's good to see you laugh, even at my expense. Anyway, the contacts I mentioned found a report of Viktor Skála's trial. You might find this bit of interest.' He pointed his finger at a slightly blurred paragraph a third of the way down the page. Slonský had to tilt the paper one way and then the other to be able to read it.

'Vitek gave evidence?'

'It was Vitek's evidence that got him convicted. He said that Skála had tried to persuade him to deliver some rifles to an address in Austria where someone would give him an envelope full of Deutschmarks.'

'And Skála was convicted on the say-so of a Prague club-owner?'

'Ah, but look at the other fax. That's from an StB commentary. Somehow Vitek had got hold of an address that they already had suspicions about. How could he know that if it wasn't true? At least, that's what they asked.'

Slonský took a long draught of his beer. 'It's all a bit messy. If Vitek wasn't working for the StB he seems to have had someone there slipping him useful information. Why would they do that?' he wondered.

'To keep them out of it. Think how it looks if all the prosecutions depend on evidence the StB say that they found. Much better if a few appear not to have anything to do with them.'

'Of course, it's all academic,' Slonský sighed. 'We now know that Skála snuffed it some time ago so he can't have been involved in getting his own back on Vitek.'

'But it opens a new line of enquiry,' Valentin insisted. 'If Vitek was prepared to do the StB's dirty work, at least where their interests coincided with his, there may be more people to hold a grudge than you might have thought.'

'The other reason why it's academic is that it's not my case. Navrátil is running it and reporting directly to Rajka on this one.'

Valentin tossed back the remains of his pear brandy. 'You've really cocked things up this time, haven't you, old friend?'

A long liquid lunch later, Slonský could no longer put off returning to his office and wearily pushed the door open. Mucha looked up at him and said nothing before returning to completing his activity log. It was Officer Fintr who came out from behind the desk to give Slonský a message.

'Major Lukas presents his compliments and asks if you would go to his office when convenient, sir.'

It was exactly the way that Lukas spoke, so there was no doubting its authenticity. He preferred invitations to orders. Slonský nodded his understanding of the message and headed for the stairs to his office.

'If I may say so, sir,' Fintr said, chasing after him to deliver his speech at low volume, 'I don't think he's very happy and you might want to go sooner rather than later.'

Slonský was not happy with the message, so he decided to bite the messenger. 'I'll go when I'm ready, Fintr.' Then, feeling that he needed all the allies he could get, he added, 'but thank you for your advice. I'll just hang my coat up and come straight back down.'

He tidied himself up and found a mint in a drawer to try to mask the smell of beer, not that Lukas would have been surprised by that. They had worked together for over thirty years, after all, including the bad years after Věra left when Slonský embarked on a close and meaningful relationship with the vodka bottle.

He plodded heavily along the executive corridor to the office that Lukas occupied right at the end. There was no secretary standing guard in the ante-room, so he approached the open door and poked his head round it, hoping to be told to go away and come back in about three weeks.

Lukas saw him. 'Captain Slonský! Thank you for coming.'

No "Josef" this time, then. It seemed unwise to point out that Slonský had only come because Lukas had ordered him to do so.

'No problem, sir.'

'Come in and shut the door.'

'Do I need a union representative here, sir?'

'I don't know, Slonský. Do you?'

'It depends what we're going to talk about.'

'We're going to talk about your actions last night. Anyway, I didn't know you'd joined a union.'

'I haven't, but I can fill an application form in really quickly if you give me a minute.'

'Sit,' Lukas commanded. 'Slonský, do you have any idea how many times I've covered for you over the years?'

'Too many to count, sir.'

'And Colonel Rajka?'

'Now and again.'

'And his predecessor, Colonel Urban?'

'Ah, now you're talking.'

'We did it because we knew that deep down you were a good policeman. Incorruptible, when many weren't.'

'So were you, sir. More so, in fact.'

'Thank you. But we're talking about you. You're capable of flashes of brilliance, unpredictable insights that crack cases open, all tempered with a genuine care for every citizen.'

'Am I getting a medal?'

'Don't push your luck, Slonský. I'm trying to get you to understand what a mess you've landed yourself in.'

'I did what I thought was right, sir. Others disagree.'

'I don't doubt that you were sincere. But you were wrong. You were sincere when you put those five hundred crowns on Slavia to win the hockey championship that time. But you were just as wrong.'

'I paid it all back,' Slonský protested. 'Eventually.'

'I know. Sincere but wrong is better than insincere but wrong. But doing the right thing would be better, don't you think?'

'Yes, sir.'

'You know that Colonel Rajka went to speak to Věra this morning?'

'Yes, sir.'

'She was extremely upset. She hardly slept because she was so annoyed with you.'

'She's good at holding grudges, sir.'

'I don't think her reaction was unreasonable, Slonský. Especially in view of one thing you said to her.'

'I regret that,' Slonský mumbled. 'That was unfair.'

'Hurrah! Some contrition at last. That has been sadly lacking.'

'If you say so, sir.'

'I certainly do. The colonel apologised on behalf of the department. She insisted that I be informed of the incident.'

'Oh, God,' muttered Slonský.

'She said that if I gave you a dressing-down, as she knew I would, and if Mucha gave you a piece of his mind, she would not make a formal complaint. If I were you, I would buy the biggest bunch of flowers I could find and leave it on her doorstep.'

'I'm not allowed to go near her, sir.'

Lukas gazed steadily at him for a few seconds before rising from his chair and collecting his coat from the rack by the door. 'I'll go with you. That'll be all right, I think.'

CHAPTER 16

The car was eerily quiet. From time to time Krob cleared his throat, and Peiperová dabbed her eyes and cheeks with a tissue. It was Jerneková who finally thought of something to say.

'It's a shame Borský doesn't have a grave, because then we could all go and pee on it.'

'All very understandable,' said Navrátil, 'but it doesn't help Gabriela one bit.'

'I'm not sure what we can do that would help her,' Krob remarked. 'At least now she's safe and she's fed regularly and gets medical care. She clearly is in no state to manage her own life.'

Peiperová rarely cried. She had attended some appalling murder scenes, seen some atrocious violence, and somehow preserved her calm demeanour throughout, but suddenly she broke into a sob. 'How can anyone do that to a young girl?'

'Because men are bastards,' Jerneková explained, quickly adding, 'present company excepted.'

'Even men don't usually do that sort of thing. Taken from home to a labour camp, your baby aborted, forcibly sterilised and all because you threaten to tell someone a man in high places has got you drunk and raped you.'

'I just hope for her sake that among the many things she can't remember, what happened to her has slipped her memory,' Krob offered.

'You must bear in mind,' Navrátil pointed out, 'that until we got there the authorities had not heard her side of the story. Her file suggested something completely different.'

'That she had been a troubled teenager with psychiatric problems?' Jerneková blazed. 'I've had that flung at me. At least I could fight back.'

'And you did,' Peiperová quickly assured her, 'and you won. Look at you now.'

Although even Slonský occasionally admitted that she was a bit of a rough diamond, there was a lot of affection within the team for Jerneková. She wore her heart on her sleeve, was fiercely loyal to her colleagues and was as brave an officer as you could find. Whether that was because her ability to assess risks correctly was questionable was another matter.

'Do you think the captain will still be there when we get back?' Krob asked.

'I don't know. Colonel Rajka was going to order him not to go to see his wife but he was too late, I gather. That's a pretty big black mark during a murder enquiry,' Navrátil answered. 'I don't see how Major Lukas will be able to avoid becoming involved, and if that happens it's only a matter of time until the captain is let go. It'll either be the sack now or a decision not to renew his contract in November. He'll be sixty-two then anyway, so that's normally the end.'

'Major Lukas is older,' Jerneková chipped in.

'Yes, but he left and then came back to fill a hole left by Rajka until someone else was ready to lead that team. He was doing the police service a favour by returning.'

'I thought you told me he was going out of his mind sitting at home with his wife and daughters?'

'I don't think I used those exact words,' Navrátil replied.

'Yes, you did. I distinctly remember.'

'I think that was Captain Slonský's description.'

'Ah, yes. I remember now.'

'Anyway, Major Lukas is talking about not asking for a renewal at the end of his year.'

'And Sergeant Mucha will be gone too. Quite a changing of the guard,' Krob said.

'I reckon I could do a good job on the desk,' Jerneková announced breezily.

'You?' Navrátil squeaked, then, realising that this may have come across as uncharitable, he continued, 'I mean, would you really like that? Your next promotion should be to lieutenant, not to sergeant.'

'Yes, but sorting out problems, making up rotas, throwing drunks into cells, I'd enjoy that. Being the public face of the police force,' Jerneková beamed. 'The first officer they see when they come in.'

Navrátil badly wanted to cross himself while driving, while Peiperová had turned quite pale. It was Krob who attempted to temper her ambition.

'I think you'd find a lot of the public rather irritating, Lucie,' he said.

'You're probably right,' she agreed. 'I find a lot of people irritating. I can't be doing with needy people.'

'You do yourself down,' Peiperová replied. 'You were compassionate towards Gabriela.'

'That's different. She's entitled to whine after what she's been through. And yet she seemed quite happy.'

'The nuns are very good with her,' Navrátil remarked. 'She feels safe with them.'

'I might have known you'd bring religion into it,' Jerneková told him. 'Not all nuns are saints. I saw one in a film a while ago whose eyes turned green and who stabbed young girls with a pointed crucifix.'

'That was fiction,' Navrátil replied.

'Yes, but it has to be plausible, or nobody would believe it.'

'I'll drop you on the corner of your street, Slonský,' Lukas said.

'Thank you. And thank you for coming with me. You didn't have to do that. I appreciate it.'

'Well, I wanted to ensure that you had the opportunity to make amends to your wife. That was a very fitting message you wrote on the card. I'm sure Věra will take it in the spirit in which it was intended.'

Slonský had written: *Sorry. I was out of order. Josef S.* on the card and tucked it between a couple of chrysanthemums. He then fished it back out again, having realised that he had not yet removed the 20 per cent off sticker that showed he had bought them at the end of the day.

'I'm sorry I had to shout at you,' Lukas said as they pulled up. 'I don't enjoy that kind of thing.'

'No, I know. I'm sorry I gave you cause,' said Slonský, and for once he meant it. Lukas was a good man. And you had to make allowances for a man with two adult daughters still living at home long after most girls had got married and moved out. He must be a stranger to his own bathroom with three women in the house, Slonský thought. They had both wondered whether Peiperová's marriage to Navrátil would give Eliška and Eva ideas about setting up their own homes, but they resolutely came home every night to see their old father — who, strange to say, seemed to love every minute of it.

The thought caused Slonský to reflect on Mucha's home life. Was it as harmonious as that of Lukas? Assuming, of course, that his sister-in-law, alias the Evil Witch of Kutná Hora, was not there. It suddenly struck Slonský that he could not remember when he last saw Mucha out of uniform. In their younger days they often went out together after work, but that had gone by the wayside when Mucha married and inexplicably preferred spending time with his wife to doing so with Slonský. For that matter, Slonský couldn't remember his wife's name, which was daft when he thought how many times he had used it over the years. It just demonstrated that maybe Mucha was not as close a friend as Slonský had long believed. In a list of close friends Slonský had always placed Mucha second, with Valentin in first place. Of course, Valentin was always available, being a bachelor, which also meant that Slonský was spared having to remember a wife's name. Their history went back as long as Slonský could remember, so far back that Slonský could not remember a time when he did not know Valentin. They had gone to school together, played truant together, provided alibis for each other, gone out with girls they didn't fancy to give their mate a chance with one he did. They were like brothers. Mucha, by contrast, only turned up during basic training when Slonský joined the police, but they immediately hit it off. Both believed in minimal effort, the difference being that Mucha did it by being very efficient, and Slonský did it by just not doing some things.

Now it was all going to end. Mucha was going to desert him. Slonský would never have done that to Mucha. If he ever thought about his last day of work, it was always going to be Mucha's last day too. They would march out of the door together, head for the nearest bar, and soothe the loss with a small lake of Pilsen's finest product.

With the excitement of the last couple of days, Slonský had forgotten all about persuading Mucha to stay. Having been removed from a major role in the Vitek enquiry, he could at least bend his brain to that for a few days. It beat signing expenses forms, anyway.

*

Morning came, and Slonský arrived punctually at seven o'clock, holding the door open so a couple of women officers could run in out of the rain. Mucha glanced up from the front desk to register who it was, then returned to writing up his log.

'Not going to say good morning to me,' Slonský asked.

'Good morning,' Mucha replied in an uninterested tone.

'Are we going to go on like this? You may want to know I took some flowers round to Věra last night to apologise.'

'Was that Rajka's idea, or Lukas'?'

'You seem to have a low opinion of me. I can be thoughtful.'

Mucha stopped writing and scrutinised Slonský closely. 'Have you had a knock on the head or do you really believe that?' he asked.

'I don't know why you're so mad at me anyway. I didn't think you liked Věra that much.'

'I don't particularly. I didn't like what she did to you. But I'm not mad about that. I'm furious that you did something so monumentally stupid that you could have been chucked out. I don't understand how you could be so dim.'

Slonský scratched his head. 'Practice, I suppose. And a natural flair for it.'

Mucha put the pen down. 'You know, when our younger one was small, I told him over and over again not to touch things because they were hot. So what did he do? I lost count of how many times we had to plunge his hand in some ice or hold it under running water. But he had the excuse that he was only four or five years old. What's yours?'

Slonský had no reply. 'I've been taken off the case,' he finally muttered.

'Good. It reduces the risk that you'll get the sack. One day you'll have to learn what you're not allowed to do.'

'I know what's right and wrong,' Slonský argued doggedly.

'Then why the hell do I have to bail you out for making the wrong choice? Can I trust you not to do it again?'

'Of course you can.'

'I wonder, I really do. Anyway, it's a shame you're off the case, because I've had a little parcel from Records. That story about Vitek recovering the money he paid to the blackmailers for the return of the explicit photographs of Maria Suková seems to be bunkum.'

'I thought as much.'

'But there is something in it. It was all a mistake, you see. It's a bit vague, but my reading is that the StB had set a trap for someone else, and the idiot of a desk clerk showed the wrong couple to the room. But when the agents saw the photos they realised all was not lost. They recognised Maria and decided they could get some money out of her.'

'Was this official or private enterprise?'

'A little side hustle they worked out. Vitek comes along and accuses them of having deliberately sabotaged the surveillance of the true target because they'd taken a bribe, and lo and behold the money was found in their possession. This is where Vitek gets clever. I'm guessing that he tells them that Suková's husband knows all about it and it's his money. If he doesn't get it back he's going to kick up a stink, so the money is given to Vitek to return to Tomáš. He will use his good offices to persuade Tomáš not to make a fuss, but he'll need to be able to assure him that those photos will never see the light of day. And they give Vitek the folder. After all, they don't need it for any investigation of their own, and they just want to draw a line under the whole thing.'

'Could one of them have finally found out what Vitek did and decided to get their own back?'

'Doubt it. Their names are in the file, but one died in 2002 and the other is banged up in prison until 2015 in connection with a murder. I've checked and he's still there.'

'Thanks. Shall I take the file upstairs?'

'There you go again. You're off the case. You can't touch it. How many times do I have to tell you these things?'

'So why did you give me the information?'

'Because you're not allowed to see the file, of course. Otherwise I'd just have let you read it.'

Having been detached from the investigation, Slonský judged it best not to sit in the office with Navrátil and Krob, but to occupy his own office next door that had once belonged to Lukas. His heart sank as he slipped into his seat and observed an in-tray full of expenses claims, memoranda to read and leave requests to process. How much better it had been when he was covering for Lukas during his illness and got Peiperová to do all the paperwork. The department had run like clockwork then. He pondered briefly asking her to do it again, but then realised that he would have nothing to do at all, and while this might be a consummation devoutly to be wished, he was acutely aware that people who are doing nothing make themselves dispensable. In the light of which, given a choice between administration and finding a crime to work on, he trotted along the corridor to see what Dvorník and Hauzer were up to.

It appeared that Hauzer was not there, though nobody liked to be dogmatic about such things given his uncanny ability to appear invisible, a boon when he was following a suspect but something of a drawback when Dvorník turned out the office lights not realising that he was still at his desk. Dvorník, however, was very much there.

Lieutenant Dvorník was the senior lieutenant by date of promotion to the role. Despite being only around five foot four inches tall, he weighed in excess of a hundred kilos, giving him a roughly spherical silhouette. His wife shared his physique, and between them they had at least eight children from a couple of marriages, who also tended towards the fuller figure. Dvorník drove them around in a minibus, and on one occasion he had passed Slonský and waved. All the children moved across to the right side of the vehicle to do likewise and Slonský could have sworn the bus tipped sideways, causing him to step smartly into a bar doorway.

'Anything going on?' Slonský asked.

'Hauzer is out looking into the theft of some candlesticks from a church,' Dvorník replied, 'and I'm writing up the evidence summary for the prosecutor about that armed robbery in the casino.'

Not for the first time Slonský reflected on the poor calibre of criminal they were up against, in this case two nincompoops who had rushed into a casino and tried grabbing all the money off the tables before realising that casino chips are not legal tender, at which point they threatened the cashier. She had used the few seconds of confusion to sound the alarm, throw all the money into the electronic safe, and slam the door. Having curled up below the counter of her little booth she had denied them a target to shoot at, which did not stop one of them having a try and making a nasty mess of the wall while also hitting himself with shotgun pellets that bounced off the bulletproof glass.

They took a hostage to try to effect an escape, but the doormen whom they had disabled with pepper spray had recovered sufficiently to hold the doors shut. When they hooked their guns over their shoulders so that they could use both hands to pull on the doors, their hostage had grabbed the guns and was holding one in each hand pointed at the thieves when the police burst in and, regrettably, fired an electrical disabling device at him. Dvorník had restricted his report to the crime itself and made no mention of this, though it was believed that Major Lukas was on the verge of issuing a reprimand to the officers involved for failure to give due warning. The thieves themselves would have got away in the confusion, except that the security staff recognised them and decided to discuss their misdemeanours at arm's length in the alley alongside, with the result that the grateful police had been given two very compliant criminals to lock up.

'Nothing I can help you with, then,' said Slonský sadly.

'No, thanks,' said Dvorník, then swiftly added, 'but can I have a word with you?'

'You already are.'

'In private.'

'There's just us here. You're not planning to ask for annual leave?' Slonský asked.

'No! Not yet, anyway. It's about my future.'

Slonský almost said *What future?* but restrained himself in the nick of time.

'The thing is — this is really awkward — I know that in a year or two you'll be retiring,' Dvorník began, then dried up.

'Don't take that for granted,' Slonský said. 'But carry on.'

'Well, you've always said I'm the senior lieutenant and I'd hoped that I'd get a crack at being the captain when the time came. Not that I'm wishing your career away.'

'Perish the thought.'

'But, then I notice you spend almost all your time with Navrátil or Peiperová and I begin to wonder if I'm going to be overlooked. Because if I am there's a job going at the moment as a firearms training officer that I like to think I'd be well qualified for and I might apply if I thought I didn't have a great future here.'

Slonský knew that if Dvorník applied to be a firearms training officer he would get the job. Dvorník was the best shot in the department, a keen member of a local gun club, and a man who could shoot an acorn out of a squirrel's paws at eighty metres. More than once Slonský had had reason to be grateful for Dvorník's skill with a weapon.

He pulled a chair across and sat down. 'Does the job come with a promotion?'

'No. I'd still be a lieutenant.'

'I spend time with Navrátil and Peiperová because I can teach them things. The fact that I don't sit on your shoulder is because I know you don't need that. It's a measure of the trust I have in you.' *That, and the fact that the others make me feel young again and laugh at my jokes*, he thought. *And Navrátil always seems to have some money on him when I forget my wallet.*

'Oh, right,' said Dvorník. 'So I don't need to worry?'

'I can't make any promises. I'll be gone when they appoint my successor after all.'

'But you can make a recommendation. They'd listen to you, if you made one.'

'Rest assured, I'll make a recommendation,' said Slonský, and winked before leaving the office.

But I've got plenty of time to decide whose name it should be, Slonský thought.

CHAPTER 17

Navrátil knocked on the door.

'It's open,' Slonský told him.

'You might be doing something private,' the young detective replied.

'With the door open?'

'On the phone.'

'I'm not holding the phone. It doesn't seem to work so well if you don't pick up that bit on the top.'

'Can I ask you a question?'

'Of course. That's what I'm here for. So long as it's not about the birds and the bees, because I get embarrassed by that stuff.'

'It's about the Vitek case.'

'I'm not allowed to get involved. You know that.'

'You're not getting involved. You're giving me helpful advice based on your experience. I'm allowed to ask for that.'

Slonský considered this for a moment, then nodded. 'That's all right then. Ask away.'

'It's like this, sir…'

'Hang on. Is this going to be a difficult question? Because, if so, we might want to get a coffee and a pastry so my brain cells are running at peak efficiency.'

'I don't think so.'

'Maybe we should get a pastry anyway, just to be on the safe side.'

Navrátil dutifully followed Slonský down to the canteen, queued behind him, decided he had better have a coffee himself, paid for both their orders since Slonský had left his wallet upstairs in his coat, and accompanied him to a table in the far corner where they would not be overheard.

'I've had another report from Spehar.'

'Ah, Technician First Class Spehar, as he's known to his friends.'

'That's him. He's managed to decipher another two names on the folders that were dyed.'

'Good for him. Speaking of being dyed, has it all washed off now?'

'Yes, thank you, sir.'

'Don't forget to claim the cost of your clothes being damaged in the course of duty on expenses, lad.'

'I have, sir. Ten days ago.'

'Have you? It hasn't come to the top of my in-tray yet. Tell you what, when we go back upstairs, feel free to go through my paperwork and plonk it on the chair. I'll see it there.'

Navrátil resisted the temptation to point out that ten days was about standard response time for paperwork submitted to his captain, and ploughed on with his question. 'These two names…'

'Neither of them is Věra Slonská, I hope?'

'No, sir.'

'Good. That damn woman gets everywhere.'

'One is Halina Veselá.'

'I know that name, but why?'

'If it's the same woman I found on the internet, she used to be a journalist.'

'Aha! She used to be a journalist, Navrátil.'

'Yes, sir.'

'It's all coming back to me. She was a dissident. Or, at least, an investigative reporter with a newspaper. I'll bet Vitek knew her. They moved in the same circles. But then she suddenly stopped writing.'

'I doubt she stopped. I think she resigned.'

'To do what?'

'I don't know, but she vanished from view. It would be good to know why.'

'You'll have to ask her, lad, if you can find her.'

'If it's the same woman, she's living in Šeberov.'

'Well, that's not too far. Just the southern edge of Prague. Go and ask her about it.'

'I will.'

'I'm glad we've got that sorted out. Come and ask me another one any time.'

'That wasn't it, sir.'

'It wasn't? There's more?'

'The second one. Jarmila Urbanová.'

Slonský pursed his lips and shook his head. 'Don't know her.'

Navrátil checked nobody was listening in before whispering his next observation. 'You know Lieutenant-General Urban, though.'

'Our boss? The Director of Police?'

'Yes. That Lieutenant-General Urban.'

'His wife?'

'I doubt it. More likely his mother.'

'You're certain about this?'

Navrátil glanced round once more before producing two photographs from his pocket. 'That's a detail from the one in Vitek's file. It's a bit blurry where they've rubbed the dye off, but you can see who it is. And this is Urban celebrating his appointment taken from the police newspaper files. That woman beside him is his mother, according to the caption.'

'Dead ringer, isn't she? You've landed yourself a corker of a conundrum there, lad.'

'What should I do about it, sir?'

'I don't know, but whatever you do, I would do it very carefully. Fortunately, I'm off this case, so it's not my call.'

'But should I tell the lieutenant-general and invite him to be present when I interview his mother?'

'Jesus Maria, no!'

'No?'

Slonský pinched his nose as if it might help him explain this. 'Get me another coffee, Navrátil, and I'll set it out for you.'

Navrátil returned with another couple of coffees. He had also picked up a pastry on the off-chance that his boss might need a bit more fuel for his brain cells.

'Why does Vitek have these folders?' Slonský asked.

'They seem to be women he has helped.'

'Exactly. They've got into trouble and turned to him to give them a bit of support. But we know at least some of them have done things that they don't want other people to know about. It's just possible that Urban's mother is one. For example, he might be the result of a one night stand with a circus performer. So if there's any risk of that, what are the chances that she would tell you with Urban sitting there?'

'I doubt that she would tell me anyway.'

'So you take a woman detective too. Fortunately, you're married to one so you've always got one on hand. Better her than Jerneková, I think.'

Navrátil flinched a little. 'I agree,' he said.

'The boss's mother had some reason to talk to Vitek, and we need to know what it is. It's as simple as that. It doesn't matter who her son is. Without fear or favour, that's our motto.'

'Yes, sir.'

Slonský pushed his chair back and stood up, patting Navrátil on the shoulder as he left. 'And if it all goes belly-up, I'll give you a good reference.'

'It just doesn't sit right with me, interviewing the director's mother without telling him,' Navrátil insisted.

'I could speak to him if you want?' Peiperová suggested. 'We got on well when I was seconded to him.'

'Would you?' said Navrátil. 'I'd appreciate that.'

'Forgive me for interrupting,' Krob butted in, 'but I think you're overthinking this. If it was any other old lady you wouldn't tell her son you were going to interview her, would you? I've never met the director, but surely he would understand that.'

'I can see that point of view,' Navrátil conceded.

'And if he knows you've talked to her he might ask her what it was about, and it might be something she doesn't want him to know,' Jerneková chipped in. 'And being top cop, he could demand to see your report, maybe even your notebook.'

'That's true,' Peiperová agreed. 'Mothers don't tell their children everything.'

Navrátil decided to be decisive, so he picked up his papers and stacked them in a tidy pile. 'Right! Let's go. Kristýna, can you come with me to see Jarmila Urbanová? Ivo and Lucie, could you interview Halina Veselá? You know what we need to ask her, don't you?'

Krob nodded.

'Great! I'll go and organise a pool car,' Jerneková said, and was gone before anyone could stop her.

Despite the team talk, Navrátil was still tense as Peiperová drove him to Mrs Urbanová's residence. It did not help that he was convinced that at any turn they might come across a wrecked police car or a scene of awful carnage outside a pavement café, but they arrived without seeing any evidence of Lucie-induced mayhem.

'I'd better introduce us,' said Navrátil, 'just in case it goes badly.'

He rang the bell, and after a few seconds they could hear the sound of someone assuring them that she was coming, if they would be patient. The door opened, and they found themselves looking at a sturdily-built woman wearing an incongruous pair of pink rubber gloves.

'Mrs Urbanová?' Navrátil said. 'We're police officers.'

'So is my son, Viktor,' she replied. 'You may have heard of him.'

'Yes, the Director of Police. We know,' Navrátil assured her.

The old lady was carefully examining Peiperová's ID. 'Peiperová? Are you the young officer who was his personal assistant?'

'That's right.'

'Yes, he said you were pretty. I hope he was a gentleman at all times or he'll be getting a piece of my mind.'

'He was, always,' Peiperová assured her. 'May we ask you some questions in connection with an enquiry?'

'Me? What can you possibly want with me?'

'It might be better if we could come in.' Navrátil suggested. 'Just in case we need to say anything confidential.'

'My son isn't in trouble, I hope?'

'Not at all. This has nothing to do with your son. In fact, it's from many years ago.'

Mrs Urbanová stood back to allow them to come in, and pointed to a room on the left. 'Please, sit down.'

Deducing that she normally sat in the chair with a small footstool in front of it, they occupied a petite sofa. Jarmila Urbanová lowered herself slowly into her chair and placed her right leg on the stool. 'I have a bit of trouble with my hip,' she explained. 'Old age, I'm afraid. My doctor says I should have it replaced, but I'm not sure I want all that fuss. Now, what's this about?'

Peiperová glanced at her husband, who motioned her to take the lead. 'We're investigating the death of a man we believe you may have known,' she explained. 'I'm sorry to have to tell you that Dominik Vitek has died.'

'Vitek? Vitek?' she mumbled.

'He ran The Ladies' Lounge in the city.'

'Oh, that Mr Vitek! What a shame. He was a kind man.'

'How did you come to know him? Were you a member of The Ladies' Lounge?'

'Goodness me, no. I could never have afforded it. We were just an ordinary family.'

'We found a folder in his safe that suggests that you had some kind of dealings with him. Could you tell us what those were?'

Mrs Urbanová shuffled uncomfortably. 'It's not easy to talk about. I'm not sure that I did the right thing. If my son knew about it…'

'Please understand that we won't tell your son what you say to us.'

'He only ever wanted to join the police. It was his dream from a small boy, and he was so proud when he was accepted. But then he started coming home in a filthy mood. I could barely speak to him without getting my head bitten off. One day his father tore him off a strip for being rude to me, and it all came out. He was angry all the time because the police service wasn't what he had been led to expect. He said a lot of his colleagues took bribes. They didn't investigate some complaints at all, and when he pointed it out they ignored him.

'Anyway, he stuck at it, and then he went up for a promotion. He was due it, everyone agreed. He worked hard, he was honest — but he didn't get it. He was ready to give it all up, because he said the officer who decided these things was one of the most corrupt ones. So long as that man was there he would never get his promotion, so he might as well give up. I begged him not to, and I did what any mother would do. I stuck up for my boy. I went to see our local city councillor. He was full of nice words but he said he and the Party couldn't interfere with the way the police ran its own business.

'Anyway, as the councillor's wife was showing me out she asked if I could come back the next afternoon. Her husband would be out then. I didn't know what she wanted, but I agreed, so the next day I was there, four o'clock on the dot. We took the bus into town and she introduced me to Mr Vitek at The Ladies' Lounge. She bought me a coffee while we were waiting. I could have had wine, but I'm not one for drinking during the day, and given what the coffee cost I dread to think what the wine must have been, yet here were all these women drinking wine and cocktails, beautifully dressed, and me in a shabby coat. It was a lovely place. So Mr Vitek invites us into his office and asks me to tell the story.'

'And you did?'

'Just as I've told you, except that I knew the name of the officer then, and it escapes me now. It was over twenty years ago, you see. Mr Vitek took some notes and my address — we didn't have a telephone then — and said he'd heard of the officer and he thought something should be done about it, but it would be best if I didn't tell my son I'd been to see him.

Well, I wasn't going to anyhow, because he'd have told me not to meddle, and I never have. And I hope you won't either.'

'No, we won't. So was Mr Vitek able to do something to help?'

'Now, in a way, I don't know, but I'll tell you what happened and you can decide for yourself. A week or more went by, and I was thinking nothing was going to come of it, when there's a knock at my door. I open it, and there's a huge man standing there. He must have been nearly six foot tall and about as wide. Dark suit, nice shirt and tie. He says Mr Vitek has sent him and it would be a good idea if my boy wasn't in the office on Thursday morning. Just that. I didn't know what to make of it, but somehow I trusted Mr Vitek and we had nothing to lose, so I made up a story about not being well and took to my bed. Viktor had to go to my work to let them know I wasn't going to be in, then to the pharmacy to get me some medicine, and a bit of shopping for our supper, and by the time he gets to work it seems he's missed all the excitement. The Security Police had been through there and taken a bunch of people away. Viktor was questioned, of course, but in the end he got his promotion. Whether Mr Vitek had anything to do with all that, I don't know, but it's a bit of a coincidence if he didn't.'

Peiperová looked meaningfully at Navrátil. It was exactly the sort of thing that Vitek seemed to have been able to pull off.

'Did Vitek expect any payment from you?' Navrátil asked.

'Payment? No. It was never mentioned. He just said maybe one day I could do a favour for him in return. I suppose that'll never happen now.'

The detectives thanked her and sat for a moment in the car before starting the engine.

'You realise what this means?' Peiperová said quietly.

'I think I know what you're going to say. Why did Vitek keep the file if he didn't expect a favour in return? And maybe he didn't get it from her, but he might have done from Lieutenant-General Urban.'

'We're going to have to talk to him.'

Navrátil nodded reluctantly. 'I'd better tell Colonel Rajka so he can make the decision.'

'Are we going to tell Captain Slonský?'

'He's off the case. And I'm reporting direct to Rajka on this one, so there's no point.'

CHAPTER 18

'No crime going on today?' said Valentin as Slonský arrived at the table with two glasses of beer.

'Probably, but none of it is coming my way. All I've got to do is sign some expenses forms, and I thought I can do that just as well here as in my office. Besides which, I knew you'd be here, and I could do with a friendly face at the moment.'

Valentin picked up one of the beers.

'Did you want one too?' said Slonský. 'Tell you what, you have that one and I'll get myself another.'

'Sorry. I naturally thought — never mind. Are you down in the dumps then?'

'Fallen out with Mucha. He shopped me for interviewing my wife. But her name came up in the case we've got on. What was I supposed to do?'

'I'm not a policeman, but by the sound of it, not that. Even journalists know you don't mix work and family. Do you want a schnapps with that? Might cheer you up.'

'Go on then.'

'So does that mean you don't give a toss whether Mucha stays or leaves now?'

Slonský looked up from his papers with a shocked look on his face. 'It never crossed my mind. No, this will pass and then we'll need Mucha. I'll just tell him what I think of him, he'll do the same to me, I'll say something smart back at him, he'll call me something abusive and we'll be best mates again.'

'Pleased to hear it. I haven't thought of any bright ideas to get him to stay, I'm afraid.'

'Me neither, and the clock is ticking. His retirement request goes in after the weekend.'

'Have you had any ideas, even dim ones?'

'Do you think he'd forgive me afterwards if I kidnapped him?'

'That might be pushing your luck a bit,' Valentin answered.

'Well, I'll be —' Slonský whispered, staring down at a form.

'Something surprising?'

'It's Hauzer. He wants to go on a leadership course. He thinks he's ready to be a lieutenant.'

'Do you think that too?'

'I've never thought about it. But I suppose he's been there a bit longer than Navrátil and Peiperová, and they've made it to that rank, so he's entitled to give it a go, I suppose.' Slonský signed the form. 'I hope he has said something to Dvorník about it. Three months is a long time to be single-handed.'

'You could bring him into one of the other teams.'

'There'd be a mutiny. Whether I add him to the men or the women, he'll outrank Navrátil and Peiperová by seniority. Maybe Rajka will let me get somebody seconded to me.'

Valentin clapped his hands. 'Mucha!'

'Mucha?'

'It would mean he has to stay around at least three months while you think of something else. And if Hauzer does well, he'll get his promotion and there'll be a permanent vacancy.'

Slonský grabbed Valentin by both ears, bent his head forward and kissed it on the top. 'It'll mean a pay rise for him. Why would he refuse?'

'You'll have to square it with Dvorník. He'd expect to pick his own team.'

Slonský laughed. 'I'll do the same to him as Lukas did to me. I'll make him an offer he can't refuse. If I hadn't taken

Navrátil, my contract wouldn't have been renewed. I'll tell Dvorník that I'll propose him as the next captain if he takes Mucha.'

'Next captain? Are you leaving then?'

'Only to go to the crematorium if I have my way. But he doesn't need to know that.'

'He might ask.'

'I'll just tell him to trust me.'

Valentin could not disguise the scepticism in his voice. 'You think that might work?'

'Absolutely. He doesn't want to move. Imagine trying to find a new house big enough for his tribe, not to mention new schools for all the little Dvorníks. Whatever he says, he has to tough it out if he wants a promotion. Oh, I feel better already! Do you fancy some sausages?'

'I could manage a little something.'

'Good. While it's coming, tell me what you know about Halina Veselá.'

'Wow, there's a name from the past! Halina Veselá! Is she dead too?'

'Not that I know of. She's living out at Šeberov the last we heard.'

'Šeberov? Next best thing to being dead.'

'But she isn't. And I can't believe you don't know something about a fellow journalist.'

Valentin took a slurp of beer to compose himself. 'She's about ten years younger than us, I'd say. Very Western, all spiky hair, skin like a goddess, mouth like a sewer.'

'Was she a good reporter?'

'She was persistent, had some good stories. Very aggressive, and her standard technique was to hold back until she had enough and then go in all guns blazing. She embarrassed a few minor figures with her exposés, then she moved on to the big guys. There was a health minister who had put his mother in a god-awful home and never visited. She was quite clever, because she didn't attack them politically; she went for their human weaknesses. The ones who drank too much, beat their wives, that sort of thing. Somehow she made contacts in the West who fed her stuff. She had a story about someone gambling in a casino in West Germany, complete with pictures. Now, she hadn't got an exit visa, so someone gave her that on a plate.'

'Western intelligence?'

'Might have been. Then one day she was gone. No more columns. I didn't see her around town, and nobody knew where she was.'

'There must have been rumours, though.'

'If there were they didn't come my way. My best guess is that she tried to bite a shark and the shark bit back.'

'I wonder who?'

'You'll have to ask her.'

'I can't. But Navrátil is on it. He'll send someone.'

To Krob's great surprise, Jerneková drove perfectly sensibly across the city to Šeberov. His heart gave a little twitch when she decided to parallel park, knowing that he was on the kerb side and that the roadside trees looked quite sturdy, but even that went well, and he was able to open the door without worrying about vegetation.

'All that practice is paying off,' he told her.

'It's easy with you. You exude calm.'

'I thought Jan and Kristýna were pretty calm too.'

'Yes, but Kristýna's my boss, so I'm always expecting criticism from her because that's her job, and Jan is so buttoned-up you never know what he's thinking. And he can pray without moving his lips, which is disconcerting when you're driving.'

Krob checked the address in his notebook. 'Number 17, apartment 2.'

'There's 15. It must be the next one.'

Calling it an apartment was a grievous misuse of the Czech language. The bungalow had been divided into two, with apartment 2 entered through what had once been the back door. A kitchenette led through to a bed-sitting room with a sofa bed, and then there was presumably a toilet and shower behind the other door.

Halina Veselá might once have been a striking woman, but many years of a rough life had left their mark. Her black hair had a couple of grey streaks, the skin over her cheekbones looked paper-thin, and her eyes were dull and sunken.

'I can't offer you anything,' she said. 'Nothing in the cupboard.'

'That's all right,' Krob replied. 'We wouldn't be allowed to accept anyway. We're investigating a death and we wondered if you could help us with our enquiries.'

'What am I getting stitched up for now?' she spat.

'You're not. It concerns a man called Dominik Vitek. While going through his papers we found a file with your name on it. We wondered if you could tell us something about your relationship with Mr Vitek.'

'Vitek? We didn't have a relationship, not a personal one anyway. For a while I belonged to that club of his for women.'

'I see. Can you put dates on that?'

Veselá shrugged. '1985, 1986.'

'The other women for whom he kept files seem to have come to him for help. Was that true for you too?'

Veselá sighed. She opened a packet of cigarettes but it was empty. 'Yes. I didn't get it though.'

'You didn't?'

'I daresay he tried, but it made no difference.'

Krob and Jerneková exchanged glances. Jerneková had written SUSPECT? in her notebook.

'Were you upset with him about that?' Krob asked gently.

'Hell, you're trying to give me a motive for killing him, aren't you?'

'We never mentioned that he'd been murdered,' Jerneková said.

'Perhaps not, but you don't investigate people dying peacefully in their sleep, do you?'

'I've got a suggestion,' Krob said. 'We'll put our notebooks down, and maybe you'd be kind enough to tell us the whole story in your own words. Then, if there's anything we need to record, we can repeat those parts.'

Veselá calmed down. 'I was a journalist. A damn good one, if I say it myself. I had some success rooting out corruption, not that you needed to be a great journalist to find that in those days. I was careful never to criticize the Communist Party so the powers that be could tell themselves that this was just a case of a few bad apples in the barrel, not due to the system itself.'

'And then?'

'Someone slipped me a folder of photos of someone gambling in a casino in West Germany and suggested I ask where he got the money from. I didn't know him at all, but it turned out he was a Deputy Minister of Finance, so you can guess where the money came from, can't you? Big success — splashed over the papers, Deputy Minister resigns but is jailed anyway, and I'm happy as a pig in — happy as a happy pig.

Then the same person gives me another lead. I start digging, and it looks very much as if someone is siphoning a percentage off the contracts he signs on behalf of the state. And this might be a small percentage, but it's big money, and it's not in Czech crowns. He has a Swiss bank account, I'm told, though I could never verify that.'

She paused, and her eyes moistened. Whatever her story was, it was still painful.

'I'd met a guy. Bit younger than me, good fun to be with. One afternoon we met up. My flatmate was good, but she was a nurse and she'd been on nightshift. I couldn't turf her out of bed so we could get it on in the other twin bed, could I? Then Petr says he can fix us up. He has a mate who works in a hotel, we can get a room for the afternoon. We pitch up, he tells me to sit in the foyer while he sorts it all out, then he comes back with a key and we go upstairs. You don't need the details of what happened next. After about an hour he's feeling thirsty, so he rings his mate to bring up some champagne. Sparkling wine, anyway. A couple of glasses and I'm feeling great, then he produces these little white tablets. He says they're all the rage in Western clubs, they expand your consciousness, that stuff. He says if you thought an orgasm was good before, wait till you do it after one of these. So we both take one, or at least I thought we both had. Either he was used to them or he didn't take it. I don't know what happened after that. It turns out when the police came I was walking round the hotel stark naked and giggling. I can't remember which room my clothes are in and the hotel staff say they can't find them anywhere, so I'm wrapped in a blanket and taken in. I sleep it off in the cells and my flatmate brings some clothes in, so I think I've blagged my way out of it.'

'But you hadn't?' Jerneková said, fairly sure that she knew what was coming next.

'No, I hadn't. A week or so later I get a parcel in my postbox, a roll of film. I don't have a projector, but I know a guy who does, so I take it to him. I've never been so embarrassed in my life.'

'It was a film of you having sex,' Jerneková announced confidently.

Veselá nodded. 'You can't see too much of Petr, but it's obvious that it's me. So I swear the projectionist to secrecy, and I take the film home and burn it. A day or two later I get a letter telling me they have plenty of copies and unless I resign by the end of the week and leave Prague they'll send a copy to my boss, to my parents, you name it. So I didn't have much choice.'

'When did you come back to Prague?'

'Even after the Wall came down I didn't dare to for a while. It was twelve years before I came back, even for a day. Then I came for a week, and finally I moved back five years ago. I thought I'd better not live in the centre where I might get noticed. I don't know where those films are. I know it wouldn't be such a sensation these days, but I'd hate one to turn up in a Prague club.'

'How do you make a living?' Krob asked.

'I work in a kindergarten. How long do you think that would last if they saw those films?'

'And where does Vitek come into this?'

'When I got the parcel and knew what was on the film, I went to Vitek because I'd heard he'd got contacts. I said I needed to get a message to whoever it was saying that I'd go quietly if they'd just give me the copies of the film. Vitek said he would see what he could do, but he only had three or four days before I had to be gone. I told him where I'd gone and he gave me some cash to rent a room and keep me going for a week or two until I could get some work. About a month later he wrote to say he wasn't getting anywhere. He knew who had ordered the film to be made but he couldn't get them to hand it over, and they'd had a still made from the film and they would get it blown up to billboard size if he kept on, so he had to admit defeat. He enclosed the photo they'd given him because he thought I should know what we were up against.' Tears rolled down her cheeks. 'It was the last time I heard from him. I kept the letter because he'd written from home instead of work.'

'You haven't kept the photo too?' asked Jerneková.

'I don't know what I did with it,' Veselá replied. 'It was all just a blur.'

'Could you find the letter?'

She pulled out an old suitcase and grabbed a bundle of letters which she examined one by one. Eventually she handed them a large manila envelope. 'That's the letter.'

Krob peeked inside. 'There's a photo in there. May we take this? I'll give you a receipt and you'll get it back.'

'I don't want it back. Just let me know when you've burned it.'

Krob and Jerneková sat in the car.

'I don't want to labour the obvious,' Jerneková said, 'but if we don't look at the photograph we won't know whether it's any help to us or not.'

'She's entitled to her privacy,' Krob said. 'I saw enough when I checked it was in there. Of course, we'll have to look at it later, but let's just get away from here, Lucie. That poor woman doesn't know who her enemy is, doesn't know if he's still alive, doesn't know if the films are still in circulation. It's a horrible way to live. I'm not going to say this very often, but put your foot down and let's get away from here.'

Jerneková obeyed, and an hour later they were back in the office. Although it was past six o'clock, Navrátil and Peiperová were still there, so they compared notes about their respective interviews. Krob produced the envelope, and they all stared at it for a few seconds before Navrátil spoke.

'We'd better see the worst, I suppose.'

Jerneková tipped the envelope up and the photograph fell on the desk. It was around twenty centimetres by fifteen, very sharp, and in full colour. 'Jesus Maria!' she exclaimed. 'That poor woman.'

Halina Veselá was in the centre of the picture, completely naked, and there were two naked men with her. They could only be seen up to their shoulders. What they were doing left nothing to the imagination.

'That's enough,' Navrátil said, and flipped the photograph over with his pen. 'Let's get it checked for fingerprints, though I doubt anything from 1986 will still be useful. Then we'll go home.'

'I need to wash my eyes with bleach,' Jerneková said.

CHAPTER 19

In the morning, Navrátil went to see Rajka to appraise him of the interview with Mrs Urbanová.

'You were quite right to interview this woman without informing the Director,' said Rajka. 'We can't treat her any differently to anyone else's mother.'

'That's what we thought, sir.'

'But on the basis of what you heard, is there any further need to trouble her?'

'No, sir. And I think she was anxious that her son should not know that she had attempted to influence his promotion.'

Rajka sat still, staring at Navrátil for some seconds. It was an odd habit of his, as if willing you to fill the silence with a confession, which Navrátil managed to resist. 'Right. I see no reason to tell him now. If he hears anything about it and tackles you, refer him to me.'

'Thank you, sir.'

'How's the case coming along?'

'I'm at a dead end, sir. We've interviewed all the women in Vitek's files, and none speak of him in any way other than admiringly. They tell us how helpful and generous he was. Far from blackmailing them, he gave several of them money. We just don't have any kind of motive.'

'Yet somebody had one, unless you believe this was a random killing.'

'Yes. And the murderer didn't seem to arouse suspicions in Vitek, who let him in.'

'But you tell me Vitek was retired. I can understand people trying to kill him twenty years ago, but why now?'

'I have no idea, sir.'

'It sometimes helps just to tell the story to someone, to help put your thoughts in order. I don't have the time at the moment, but I could make an hour or two tomorrow. Before then, why not run it past Captain Slonský?'

'I thought you said I wasn't to involve him, sir.'

'I said I wanted you to decide how much to involve him. And I still don't want him near witnesses. But he's a fine detective with lots of experience, and perhaps he can suggest other lines of enquiry. On top of which, I happen to know he's bored out of his skull and a bored Slonský is a pest to us all.'

Slonský had run out of things to sign or refuse. He had been to give Hauzer the good news about his training course, but Dvorník was out on an enquiry so he would have to wait until later to hear the good news that Slonský planned to foist Mucha on him without, of course, asking Mucha first.

He was now loitering in the canteen for prolonged periods. He had already suggested a couple of changes of layout to Dumpy Anna designed to improve the catering department's efficiency, and had questioned whether it was really necessary to give vegans so much choice, since there was only one now that woman from Family Court Liaison had gone on maternity leave. They could just ring the remaining vegan and ask what he wanted them to make each day.

'Haven't you got any work to do?' Dumpy Anna asked, slicing the liver sausage a little thicker than usual for him.

'Done it all. We've run out of crime. It's a terrible position for a police force to be in.'

'You'll feel guilty taking your salary this month,' she told him.

'I wouldn't go quite that far. If I don't take my salary I can't spend it all in here, can I?'

'Speaking of which, I see you're wearing your coat.'

'Yes. And?'

'So your wallet will be in it and you can clear your tab. I'm not supposed to give credit anyway.'

'That's why I get Navrátil to pay. But I don't want to get you into trouble. How much is it?'

Dumpy Anna produced a small cash book from her pocket and turned to the back page. 'Three hundred and fourteen crowns.'

'How much? I'm not clearing everyone's tab.'

'Nobody else has a tab. Look, there are five coffees, one bratwurst, two sandwiches…'

'I believe you. There you are. Keep the change.'

'You're five crowns short.'

'Am I?'

They counted the money together, and Slonský sheepishly made up the difference. 'Sorry about that, Anna.' He picked up his tray but she held it down with her chubby hand and flipped a croissant onto his plate alongside the sandwich. They both smiled.

Krob was re-reading the file, yet again, when something occurred to him. He looked once more at Navrátil's notes on the interview with Věra Slonská, then took them next door to discuss them with Slonský.

'I'm not allowed to have an opinion on this,' Slonský said, 'whatever it is that you're going to tell me.'

'I just wanted to ask you if you mentioned The Ladies' Lounge when you spoke to your wife.'

'It all got a bit heated. I can't remember. But I don't think I did. I asked her how she knew Vitek.'

'Maybe she doesn't. Maybe she has a connection to the place, not the man. The StB saw her leaving or something of that kind, put two and two together and made five.'

'It wouldn't be the first time. Do me a favour, Krob. Go and put that to her. Have you got the address?'

'It's on the statement, sir. Should I wait for Lieutenant Navrátil to get back?'

'No, lad. Slip out while it's quiet.'

The reason that Navrátil was not in the office was that he had an appointment. Reasoning that there were some things that others did not need to know about, he had put some private enquiries in train which had borne fruit, and he was on his way to meet someone at half-past nine to take her for a little drive.

Jakub Petrák's daughter Jana was waiting on the corner as she had promised. She was in her mid-forties, he estimated, wearing a coat that had probably fitted a little better a couple of years ago and some boots with worn-down heels. She looked nervous.

He pulled up, ran round to open the car door, and closed it again once she was safely in her seat. 'You're sure you're happy to go through with this?' he asked.

'Yes,' she said, although the catch in her voice suggested some residual reservations about the whole idea.

'He's not well, but he wanted to see you. You'll have a lot to talk about.'

'Yes. It's been a while. He wasn't the best dad.'

'But he's not long for this world, I'm afraid.'

'I know. And if he died and we'd left things unsaid I'd feel guilty. He's still my father.'

'I'll take you in, then once you're happy I'll leave the two of you to chat. I'll wait outside. Take as long as you want. If I have to go I'll tell you and arrange a taxi to take you back.'

Jana smiled weakly. 'You're very kind. It's a shame my brother isn't around to come too.'

Navrátil had not realised that he was dead. 'I'm sorry,' he said. 'What happened to him?'

'Eight years for armed robbery.'

Věra was less than thrilled to have another visitor. 'Am I going to meet the whole damn department?' she asked.

'I realise this is tiresome for you,' Krob said, 'but I think I might have an answer as to why you were in the StB's files. Forget the man, Mr Vitek. Did you ever go to The Ladies' Lounge?'

Věra frowned. 'Goodness, that's going back a bit! I couldn't afford that sort of place. But I did go a handful of times when they wanted casual waitresses or bar staff. One of my friends worked there and tipped me off that work was going.'

'Vitek owned it.'

'Did he? I never met him. I only ever answered to the woman who managed the staffing.'

'Did you do any jobs that took you outside?'

Věra thought hard. 'Maybe a bit of shopping if they needed milk or sugar. A couple of times when they asked me to push an envelope through someone's door.'

'I don't suppose you remember which door?'

'I haven't a clue. It wasn't written on the envelope. I had to memorise it so I used to write the number on my hand just in case I forgot, because they said it was very important that it went to the right door. And I had to knock when I delivered it but then leave at once before anyone answered.'

Krob smiled. 'Vitek was using you as a courier. He daren't do it himself, so he'd send someone innocent to do it for him who could plausibly deny any knowledge if she was stopped. My guess is that the StB were watching that door and followed up to see who you were.' He zipped his jacket up and held out a hand. 'Thank you. I think we can guarantee you won't be bothered any more about this.'

'In that event, I'm glad you came.'

Krob paused. 'Did you like working at the Lounge?' he asked.

'Not really. Most of the women were fine, but you'd get one or two who would make ... suggestions. I wasn't comfortable with that. I mean, if you work in a bar in town then you'd get used to having your bottom groped by men, but having it groped by women is quite a different thing.'

Peiperová had also had a brainwave. That little slip of paper with a number on it in Ditka Hrubešová's file had been bugging her. There were no transactions in Vitek's bank account that might relate to rental of a lock-up. So who, she asked herself, would let you keep something locked up with no obvious transaction charge? She could think of only two answers; a pawnbroker — but there was no name and address to retrieve the item and they had not found any receipt — or his bank. She rang the bank and quoted the number to the manager, who told her that the G at the front might be a badly written nine, in which event the box could indeed be one of theirs. He would need a warrant to allow her access, but he would be glad to do so if she brought one along.

Thanks to Major Klinger, who had applied for many of these over the years, she soon had the piece of paper in her bag and arrived at the bank with a receipt book and a large evidence bag. Shown to the vault, she waited as the manager carefully read the warrant, checked the number on the slip against the bank's register of holders, confirmed that Mr Vitek had hired it and handed her the key.

Peiperová pulled the drawer open carefully, mindful of what had happened to her husband, but there was no explosion. Instead, she found herself looking at bundles of letters tied with pieces of string, some envelopes full of photographs, and a couple of rolls of 8mm film. She dutifully made an inventory of the contents and had a photocopy made for the bank, but decided that if the photographs and films were what she thought they were, she would not allow the bank manager to see them. Fighting against her natural curiosity, she transported the unopened bag back to her desk, collected a cup of coffee, and gingerly opened the first envelope.

The contents were surprisingly tame. They looked like surveillance pictures taken through bushes in a park, and showed a man and a woman in what looked like 1970's clothing taking a walk together.

The second envelope was quite different, so much so that she jumped a little as she saw what the images depicted. It was only when she found the sixth photograph that she recognised it as the photograph that Maria Suková had verified as being of her and the intern, so presumably the others were also part of that set, in which event she was not surprised that Suková had wanted them found and destroyed.

The third envelope was of a similar kind, but there were two men in some of the pictures, and it was immediately obvious that the woman in the picture was Halina Veselá. Perhaps the film was also of her, she thought, and unwound a couple of metres to hold it up to the light. Given the size of each frame she could not be sure, but it seemed likely. She locked the other material in her desk, picked up the rolls of film, and set out for the laboratories where she would ask Spehar to have copies made on video so they could view it without risking damaging the original evidence.

Spehar immediately put a technician onto the task, and an hour or so later Peiperová was on her way back to her desk, so excited that she completely forgot about lunch. Jerneková was lounging in her chair with her feet up on the desk, dipping a pickle in sour cream and slurping it off.

'Better than a spoon,' she explained. 'You can't eat a spoon at the end.'

'Anybody else around?'

'The men are in the canteen, I think. Your husband's been out with a woman.'

'I beg your pardon?'

'Not like that. He smells of cheap scent and he deflects the questions when you ask what he's been doing. And he blushes. It's quite cute, really.'

Peiperová ran down the stairs and found Navrátil, Krob and Slonský sharing a table. Navrátil and Krob had finished eating, while Slonský was debating whether to have the cinnamon bun or the poppy-seed roll next.

'I hear you've been out,' she said as levelly as she could.

'That's right,' chorused Krob and Navrátil.

'You went together?'

'No, I went to see Mrs Slonská,' Krob told her. 'I think we've tidied that loose end up. She worked occasionally at The Ladies' Lounge.'

'I see,' Peiperová said, then, observing that her husband was not being forthcoming about his own outing she gave him a prod. 'And you?'

'I just went out to see Mr Petrák again.'

'Does he wear a lot of jasmine, then?'

'Pardon me?'

'You smell of jasmine,' Peiperová said.

'Yes, I noticed that,' Slonský agreed, 'but I didn't like to mention it because Navrátil is entitled to keep a bit of mystery about him.'

By now Navrátil had the appearance of an overripe tomato. 'I took his daughter to see him.'

'His daughter?'

'They've been estranged a long time. But he's dying, so she agreed to meet up.'

'Why be so secretive about it? It's a nice thing to do.'

'It's their private business. No need to make a song and dance about it all.'

Slonský smiled. 'Oh, lad, you've no idea what Kristýna was thinking, have you?'

'Thinking? About what?'

'You don't tell anyone where you're going, disappear for most of the morning and come back smelling of perfume and it doesn't occur to you that your wife might have suspicions?' Slonský chuckled.

'It wasn't just me,' Peiperová pointed out. 'Lucie thought the same.'

'Ah, but Lucie is prepared to think ill of anyone,' Slonský said. 'And usually with good cause. Whereas those of us who have known Jan longer know that your husband only has eyes for you, and what big puppy eyes they are too when your name is mentioned. Anyway, where have *you* been, and why do you smell of dust and damp carpet?'

'I've been to Vitek's bank, and I've collected the contents of his deposit box there.'

'Have you indeed? And pray tell, what were they?'

'A lot of letters, three sets of photographs, including one lot of Maria Suková and another lot of Halina Veselá, and a couple of rolls of film that Spehar has transferred to video so we can watch them.'

Slonský frowned. 'I can't watch that kind of thing on a full stomach. You three go ahead and I'll join you later.'

CHAPTER 20

There are circumstances in which watching erotic videos might be quite exciting, but a police office in the early afternoon was not one of them. Navrátil found them extremely educational because there were things going on of which he had no experience, whereas Krob contented himself with making occasional notes with a stopwatch so that they could find the relevant scene again. Jerneková kept up a running commentary between bites of pickle. Peiperová suggested that they only needed to watch enough to identify the people concerned.

'How do you know someone else doesn't turn up later?' asked Slonský.

'Sorry, sir. I didn't hear you come in,' Peiperová replied.

'No, you were completely engrossed in this filthy exhibition. By the way, I do not want to find this being shown in a back room at the police Christmas social.'

'That never crossed our minds, sir,' Navrátil assured him.

'I can certainly believe it wouldn't cross yours, lad, but there are precedents. Anything interesting in these pictures?'

'It's Halina Veselá and her boyfriend. The other one hasn't turned up yet,' Navrátil replied.

'If you ask me, he knows the cameras are there,' Jerneková opined. 'Look how he turns sideways on a lot of the time so we don't see him full face.'

'Can we just freeze the film a moment?' Krob suddenly asked. He ran to his desk to fetch a photograph. 'Look at the curtain tiebacks. The one on the right isn't properly lined up with the one on the left, see? It looks like it's been bent or dislodged a bit. Now look at the photograph we found in Maria Suková's file.'

'It's the same,' Slonský declared. 'It's the same room.'

'The furniture is different,' Peiperová pointed out.

'Furniture is easily changed. Hotels do it all the time. They put in an extra bed, take out a bed, put in a child's crib and so on. This room — what was it?'

'Room 305, sir,' Krob supplied.

'Whoever interviewed Maria Suková before, get onto her and see if she can remember which hotel it was. Well done, Krob.'

Krob was not paying much attention. Ignoring the others, he was crouched by the screen with a ruler in his hand.

'Krob, if you're measuring what I think you're measuring it betrays a sense of insecurity you don't want to own up to,' Slonský told him.

'I'm not measuring that,' came the reply. 'Do you see the scar just above the knee? It's on this picture too. It's the same man.'

Slonský pushed him aside to check for himself. 'Jesus Maria, so it is! We can't see his face too well, but that hook-shaped scar is pretty unique, I'd say.' He sat on the corner of Navrátil's desk, which caused the far end to elevate, so he leaped to his feet again. 'Fork-lift trucks!' he exclaimed.

There was an awkward silence for a moment.

'Is that a euphemism?' Jerneková asked.

'It's something Major Grigar said the other day. He was reminiscing about thefts from some factory or other. A guy kept driving out with a fork-life truck and they were sure he was stealing something, but he always had permits for everything he was shifting. The point is…'

'He was stealing the fork-lift trucks,' Navrátil completed.

'That's it. We've been looking at the wrong thing. Who interviewed Maria Suková?'

'Lucie and I did,' Peiperová said.

'Then get out there and ask her to come in for a chat. She knows more than we've asked her so far.'

'And if she won't come?' Peiperová asked.

'Arrest her.'

'On what charge?'

'I don't know. Improvise. Accessory to murder if need be. Just get her in here.'

The women left the room. Navrátil cleared his throat.

'You wanted something, lad?'

'I just thought I should point out, for your own good, that it's my enquiry and you're banned from playing a part.'

'Quite right. And if you don't want to solve it by all means run along the corridor to Colonel Rajka and turn me in. If you know the right questions to ask that's fine, but if not, at least let me be in the room. You can take the lead. I'll just fill the gaps.'

'If it was up to me, sir, I'd be okay with that, but…'

'Come on. Let's see Rajka.'

The colonel listened carefully to Slonský's explanation.

'What makes you think that Lieutenant Navrátil doesn't know what to ask?'

'He might. But he might not. I'm not asking to take the case back, just to be allowed in the room while he questions Ms Suková. And we may as well add in Ms Veselá too, because she'll be next.'

'If I gave permission, would you be comfortable with that, Lieutenant?'

Navrátil was standing to attention for some reason that presumably made sense to him. 'Yes, sir. But it's still my case.'

'Of course it is,' said Rajka.

'Nobody said otherwise,' Slonský agreed.

'The catch is,' Rajka continued, 'that there really should be a female officer in the room too, given the sensitive nature of the material you'll be discussing, and I think three officers to one witness is one too many.'

'You'll have to let Peiperová take your place, lad,' Slonský immediately declared.

'It's my case,' Navrátil replied with spirit. 'You'll have to stand down.'

'How can I stand down when I'm the one who knows the questions?'

'Tell me the questions you want answering and I'll make sure I ask them.'

'How do I know what the questions are before I've heard the answers to the other questions?' bellowed Slonský.

'Gentlemen!' Rajka interrupted. 'I have an idea. If Ms Suková does not object, Lieutenant Peiperová could sit beside her to offer some support. Lieutenant Navrátil will sit opposite, and Captain Slonský will sit at the back of the room and ask Lieutenant Navrátil for permission to ask any supplementary questions he thinks fit. Is that understood?'

'Perfectly, sir,' said Navrátil.

Slonský scratched his head. 'So I'm in the room, but not at the table?'

'Correct,' Rajka confirmed.

'But I can talk?'

'With the lieutenant's permission. Which, of course, he will not unreasonably withhold.'

Slonský seemed to be having trouble visualising this configuration, but since it was this or nothing, he declared himself satisfied.

'Good,' said Rajka. 'Let's hope you can bring this one home now.'

Maria Suková made no objection to coming in once she had satisfied herself that the car that Peiperová had parked across the street was an unmarked police car.

'I wouldn't want the neighbours to see me apparently being arrested,' she said.

'Given the size of your garden, your neighbours would need pretty good eyesight to see anything,' Jerneková answered.

They clambered into the car, Peiperová driving, Jerneková alongside her, and Suková in the back. Peiperová started the engine.

'Check the rear-view mirror, turn on left turn indicator, pull out smoothly,' Jerneková recited.

'I know,' said Peiperová. 'I *can* drive.'

'No, I'm just going through the motions for my benefit,' Jerneková said.

'Could you do it silently?'

Jerneková looked stunned, as if such an idea would never have occurred to her, but complied. This was not the end of the distractions, however. At intervals she moved her hands and feet as if applying the brake, accelerating or changing gear.

Maria Suková was ushered into the interview room, and Peiperová was invited to stay in accordance with Rajka's instructions.

'Lucie,' said Navrátil, 'Ivo is waiting to take you to collect Halina Veselá and bring her in.'

'Can't I stay for the juicy bit?'

'We can't all be in the room. Besides which, you and Ivo interviewed her in the first place.'

Jerneková was about to pout, until an idea hit her. 'Can I drive?'

'Negotiate that with Ivo.'

Jerneková bounded off along the corridor, and Navrátil entered the interview room to find everyone already sitting in their allocated places. Slonský had his back to the wall behind Navrátil, who could not see him without turning round. He began to suspect that Slonský had deliberately placed himself there so that he could not be watched.

'Thank you for coming in,' Navrátil began politely. 'I'm Lieutenant Jan Navrátil, I believe you already know Lieutenant Peiperová, and behind me you can see Captain Slonský, who is our superior.'

Maria Suková leaned to one side so that she could see Slonský, who waved back.

'I'll be conducting this interview, but Captain Slonský may chip in if he can help us get to the bottom of this.'

'Absolutely,' Slonský agreed. 'Pretend I'm not here. Most of the time.'

'If the questions become uncomfortable, please say so. We have no wish to cause you any distress.'

'Absolutely not,' Slonský agreed. Spotting Navrátil turning towards him, he added, 'But pretend I'm not here.'

'We're not interviewing under caution. You're here voluntarily as a witness.'

Slonský came to the table. 'Just turning the tape recorder on,' he explained. 'Pretend I'm not here.'

'Thank you,' Navrátil said. He remained patient and in control but was unsure how long that feeling would last. 'Now, Ms Suková —'

'Testing, one, two, three, four,' boomed Slonský. 'That's fine, it's recording.'

'Thank you, sir. Lieutenant Jan Navrátil interviewing Ms Maria Suková. Captain Josef Slonský and Lieutenant Kristýna Peiperová are also in the room.' He announced the date and time, causing Slonský to adjust his watch. 'Ms Suková, we have managed to find a cine film and some photographs relating to an incident in 1986.'

'A cine film?' Maria asked weakly.

'I'm afraid so. It seems that at some point Mr Vitek was able to trace and secure these.'

'And he didn't tell me?'

'I can offer no explanation for that, I'm afraid. They were in a safety deposit box at the bank and had been there about ten years, which would suggest he obtained them about 1999.'

'Though he may have had them somewhere else before then,' Slonský added.

'We don't know that,' Navrátil said, a little louder than he intended.

'Absolutely not,' agreed Slonský.

'I'm afraid I have to ask you to identify the photographs,' Navrátil said, sliding them, face down, across the table. Suková cautiously lifted the corner of each and lowered her head to examine them.

'Yes,' she said, 'those are the photographs I was blackmailed over. Why didn't they offer the film too? Did they always intend to circulate that?'

'I have a theory about that,' Slonský said, but, seeing Navrátil turning towards him once more, swiftly added, 'but I'll save it until later.' It was at this point that it dawned on Slonský that if he just watched the expression on Peiperová's face he could work out what Navrátil was thinking.

'We have ascertained that the hotel room in question was used on more than one occasion to entrap a woman in this way. Can you tell us where it was?' Navrátil asked.

'I'm not altogether sure. Somewhere along Jindřišská, I think. The city has changed so much since 1986.'

'Of course. Let's talk about your companion. What can you tell us about him?'

'His name was Petr. I'm not sure of his surname now. Chválek? Something like that. He was an intern at the ministry, a student at the university who was taken on to give him some real world experience.'

'Do you know how old he was?'

'Maybe twenty-two, twenty-three. He was assigned to my team. He was clearly ambitious, and had a good head for figures. I set him to preparing some briefing papers for a conference of Eastern Bloc finance ministers, and since he had the best grasp of them he was added to the delegation. We spent a few days in Poland. He was polite, presentable and attentive, and my head was turned. The conference centre had a swimming pool. He suggested we had a swim together one evening. One thing led to another and after dinner ... well, we got to know each other better.'

'And it continued when you returned to Prague?'

'I thought it was just one of those holiday romances you read about, but a couple of days later we found ourselves alone in my office and said how much fun we'd had, and that was when he mentioned the hotel. One afternoon we had a meeting at the castle and since it finished early and we wouldn't be missed we went to the hotel. You know the rest.'

'After the encounter at the hotel, you received the blackmail letter. What was Petr's response to that?'

'He was shocked. He said he hadn't had anything of the kind, but then who would be interested in an intern? He was very apologetic that he had got me involved in it, but we agreed we had to end it then, and he said since seeing me every day would be difficult for him, perhaps he should see if he could transfer somewhere else. I haven't seen him since.'

'He'll have changed over twenty-three years,' Slonský said. 'He'll be in his mid-forties. You might not recognise him if you came across him. Did he have any distinguishing marks?'

'He had a scar near his knee. I noticed it when we were swimming. Someone skated into his leg when he was playing hockey and he fell over on the ice.'

'Thank you,' said Navrátil. 'I think we're done here — unless Captain Slonský has any more questions?'

'No,' beamed Slonský. 'I think you've asked everything.'

'What will happen to the photographs and film?' Suková enquired.

'We'll have to retain them as evidence for the time being. But rest assured they'll be kept securely. In due course they may be destroyed. I'm assuming you wouldn't want to claim them?'

'I just want to know they've been destroyed as soon as possible.'

'You asked why the film wasn't shown to you,' Slonský interrupted. 'I think it's because photographs are easily developed whereas cine film takes a bit longer. They maybe just didn't have it to hand when they decided to blackmail you. But no doubt it would have surfaced in time if Mr Vitek hadn't rescued you.'

'Do you know how he was able to identify the blackmailers and retrieve the photographs?' Suková asked.

Navrátil decided that he would let Slonský answer that one.

'There are a number of possibilities. The story he told you was bunkum. The blackmailers were not involved in a mysterious car crash. Either he knew who did this sort of thing, or they contacted him and he bought them as he said, or perhaps he was part of the gang.'

'Vitek? Surely not!' Suková snapped.

'I think that's speculation,' Navrátil said.

'Of course,' agreed Slonský. 'Not a shred of evidence. Just trying to be exhaustive about the possibilities. I'm just going to splash my boots. Don't start the next interview without me.'

Halina Veselá was at work when Krob and Jerneková called, but they waited for her outside the kindergarten and brought her in. Navrátil was feeling guilty that Peiperová had not played a leading role in the enquiry so he suggested that she should lead the interview while he wrote up the notes on the previous one. Jerneková naturally assumed that she would be the second officer, and was a bit put out when Peiperová suggested that Krob needed the experience, which was a polite way of saying that the prospect of having Jerneková interrogating people was one that set her teeth on edge. Navrátil smoothed the matter over by proposing that, as for Suková's interrogation, they should have a female officer on the other side of the table to offer empathy.

'Empathy? I can do that,' Jerneková announced brightly, leaving Slonský momentarily at a loss for words, but soon the team were reassembled in the interview room. Slonský's chair had somehow wandered a couple of metres closer to the table.

Peiperová effected introductions and turned the recorder on, thus leaving Slonský hovering halfway between his seat and the table with one hand dangling in mid-air.

'We have retrieved a cine film and some photographs relating to a historic blackmail attempt,' Peiperová began.

'It wasn't an attempt,' Veselá protested. 'It succeeded.'

'Thank you for the correction. Can you put a date on the incident?'

'It was late in May 1986. I can't tell you the exact date.'

'What about the location? What do you remember of that?'

'It was a hotel in one of the streets behind Na Příkopě. Maybe Jindřišská? I'm not sure.'

'Let's turn to the men.'

'Men?'

'The two men.'

'I don't remember two men — just Petr.'

Peiperová searched the file for a photograph but before showing it to Veselá she prepared her for a surprise. 'The cine film shows two men. They must have sent you an edited version, perhaps just the start.' She offered Veselá the photograph, who glanced at it briefly before handing it back with a disgusted look on her face.

'I want you to know I'm not the sort who would do that kind of thing. It was only because I'd been drugged.'

'We understand that,' said Peiperová.

'It's not consensual if you're out of your head,' Jerneková added.

'I don't know who the second man is,' said Veselá.

'Let's concentrate on the other one, then,' Peiperová continued. 'What can you tell us about him?'

'I met him at a poetry recital. He introduced himself, wanted to buy me a drink, so we went to a bar. He knew where a party was going on — he always seemed to know of a party — and we went on. I had a good time and agreed to meet him again a few days later. We slept together for the first time a few days after that.'

'His place or yours?' Slonský interjected.

'Mine. My flatmate was out. I never went to his place. I don't even know where he lived. He only told me he still lived with his parents.'

'How did this encounter at the hotel come about?' Peiperová wanted to know.

'We met up for lunch. He couldn't make a date that evening, but my flatmate was sleeping so we couldn't go there, and that's when he said he knew of a place where we could go.'

'So he made the running?'

'Yes. He collected the key, like I said the other day.'

'And there was nothing in the room to arouse your suspicion?'

'No. we were told we could have it until seven o'clock. Nobody had reserved it that evening.'

'And at some stage Petr slipped you a drug?'

'He didn't slip it to me. He offered it and I took it willingly. I thought he'd taken it too. Maybe he did, but it didn't affect him like it affected me.'

'Do you remember how you came to be naked in the corridor?'

'No idea at all. I felt really excited and everything was great until it wasn't. About four hours must have gone by that I know nothing about.'

'What was Petr's surname?'

'Chvátal. Petr Chvátal.'

Slonský interrupted again. 'Not Chválek?'

'No, definitely Chvátal.'

Slonský excused himself and left the room, racing through to the foyer to catch Mucha before he went off duty. 'Can you do me a favour?' he asked.

'Do I need to hang my coat up again?'

'It'll be a few minutes for a man of your abilities.'

'You reckon? What is it?'

'That database you get into that has lists of StB agents. I'm looking for one called Petr Chvátal.'

'The politician?'

'I don't know anything about a politician. The one I'm after is a drug-supplying pervert,' Slonský mumbled.

'Yes, that'll be the one,' said Mucha.

'You've heard something?'

'No, but it just rings true. Don't you read the papers?'

'Just the sports pages and what's on the television.'

'I didn't think you watched television?'

'No, but it's good to know what I'm missing in case I don't want to miss it.'

'So why have you got a television if you never watch it?'

Slonský shrugged his shoulders. 'It gives me somewhere to put my breakfast down while I put my shoes on.'

'Did you at least know there's a vote of no confidence in the Prime Minister next week?'

'I'm not surprised. But no.'

'And if he loses there may be a general election. But in any event there'll be one next year. There's a Petr Chvátal who leads the Family and Tradition Party.'

'The what?'

'The Family and Tradition Party. It's a bit like the old Christian Democrats except that it's not explicitly religious.'

'I can't keep track of all these new parties springing up all the time. Is he likely to win?'

'The polls say he hasn't a snowball's chance in hell. Might not even get elected himself. But he can dream.'

'The label "Family and Tradition" suggests that they stand for old-fashioned family values.'

'Anti-abortion, anti-divorce, support for traditional Czech industries.'

'If that includes brewing I might vote for him. Unless he's a drug-supplying pervert, of course.'

Mucha nudged Fintr out of the way so he could get to the computer terminal. 'Turn your back while I put my password in.'

'I wouldn't steal your password,' Slonský complained. 'I've got my own password.'

'And do you know it?'

'Of course not. I've got it written down in a locked drawer of my desk. I just don't know where the key's gone.'

'Right, we're in. Chvátal, Petr. There you go!'

Slonský quickly scanned the record. 'He's not known to have been with the StB for long.'

'From 1985 to 1989, then they got wound up in 1990.'

'He got out before the Wall fell.'

'We don't know that. We only know that he wasn't given any jobs after 1989.'

'Does it tell us what he did?'

'Not much. Quite a big bonus payment in 1986, but it doesn't say what for.'

'I know what for. Thanks.'

'Am I hearing things?' Mucha said. 'Did you just say thanks?'

'Yes.'

'To me?'

'Yes. I appreciate all you do. I'll miss you when you're gone.'

'Will you?' said Mucha, putting his coat back on. 'Well, you'll have to wait a while.'

'What?'

'I'm not going.'

Slonský gave serious thought to giving Mucha a hug, but restrained himself. 'You said you were going to retire.'

'I can't, can I?'

'Can't you?'

'And leave you to get into seven kinds of trouble every week? If this case has proved anything, it's that you don't know how to keep yourself on the straight and narrow. I need to stay until you get through to retirement without getting yourself suspended or sacked.'

Slonský opened his mouth to protest but then realised that any argument on his part might cause Mucha to change his mind. He had what he wanted. Let that be enough.

Navrátil listened carefully to Peiperová and Slonský.

'So you're saying this fellow Chvátal was recruited by the StB as a young man, and now that he's trying to get into parliament he doesn't want word of his StB activities to leak out.'

'Got it in one,' Slonský insisted. 'That's why Vitek kept the films. It wasn't to threaten the women. It was to get revenge on Chvátal if he ever crossed his path. When Chvátal formed his family values political party, Vitek must have told him to forget all about it or he would release the films. Chvátal went to Vitek's apartment to try to talk him out of it, it turned nasty, and Vitek was killed.'

'But why did Vitek let him in?' Navrátil asked.

'He didn't see a threat. Logically, Vitek knew the films weren't there, so why would Chvátal harm him? If he did, he'd never find out where they were. The problem was that Chvátal thought they must have been there, so the deterrent didn't work.'

'Even if this is all true,' Navrátil noted, 'it's circumstantial. How can we place Chvátal at the scene of the crime? We'll never get a conviction with what we've got.'

'Then we need to employ cunning, lad. We need to convince Chvátal that we've got a lot more. We've got to get him to confess.'

'And how do we do that?'

'I'll have to have a think. And in order to have a good think I'll have to have a beer. Although, if Chvátal's such a fan of tradition, we could try getting one in the traditional way — by opening a top-floor window and inviting him to take a closer look at the view.'

'Those days are gone, sir.'

'I know, Navrátil. But it was effective. You had to do it at the back of the building, of course. Dangling people from a window over the street in front was just asking for trouble.'

Krob had been despatched to see if Spehar's team could prove that Chvátal had been in or near Vitek's apartment, but Spehar was sceptical.

'We can extract location data, and he probably didn't turn his phone off so we'll be accurate to within tens of metres, but we don't know when the murder took place and, given that Vitek lived close to the centre of the city, the chances that anyone was nearby will be very high. Half the population of Prague were probably within range at some time in the past few weeks.'

Dr Novák was not much more helpful. 'I can tell you from the forensic entomology that he had been dead between eleven and twenty-two days before he was found.'

Krob could not really see that this advanced their prospects of a conviction much, but on re-reading Novák's report he noticed a lead that had not been followed up. Reasoning that someone who often goes out for a meal probably does not go far much of the time, he took a photograph of Vitek and tramped around the restaurants and cafés of that part of Prague. There were a large number, but he could discount any that would not serve tripe.

Eventually he struck lucky, or his persistence paid off. He came across a small family restaurant in a back street that had tripe on the menu.

'Mr Vitek? Yes, he often came here. He liked tripe. Not a favourite of mine, I have to admit,' said the owner, 'but he said it reminded him of his childhood.'

'I don't suppose you recall him coming in to have tripe in February?' Krob asked.

'I can do better than that — I can tell you the exact day. We don't take holidays in mid-summer because we lose too much trade, but we take a week off in February and shut up shop. And on our first day back, there's Mr Vitek waiting for his tripe. Saturday, 14th February.'

'You're sure of that?'

'Yes. We aren't going to take a day off on Valentine's Day, are we? We actually came back on the Friday but we had to get some food delivered.'

'Did he pay with a credit card?'

'No, always cash.'

'And I don't suppose he made a booking.'

'No, just turned up at midday when we started serving lunch. He hasn't been in since. Has something happened to him?'

'I'm afraid he died later that same day. That's why we're trying to find out where he ate so we can fix which day it was.'

'That's fine so far as it goes,' said Krob, 'but it doesn't help us link Chvátal to the crime.'

'Never mind, lad,' said Slonský. 'It's good work nonetheless.'

Peiperová was the next to have an idea. 'Sir, if Vitek kept the films and Chvátal comes to see him to snatch them back, how does Vitek know how to contact Chvátal and how does Chvátal know where Vitek lives?'

'Those are good questions, lass. So answer them. What are the possibilities?'

'Well, nobody we've spoken to seems to know exactly where Vitek lived. One of the women knew he'd moved nearer to the National Theatre, but he seems to have guarded his privacy. So if Chvátal found him, unless he had access to an official computer then Vitek must have told him.'

'Surely Vitek would meet in a public place? It would be much safer.'

'But they might be overheard.'

'That matters to Chvátal, but Vitek wouldn't give two hoots about that. He has nothing to hide.'

'Don't political parties get to see voter lists?' asked Jerneková.

'I don't know,' Slonský admitted. 'But I wouldn't be surprised if they can ask around their local branches to see if anyone knows a particular voter.'

'But Vitek must have been able to contact Chvátal first,' persisted Peiperová.

'And if he did, he wouldn't want to leave anything permanent because Chvátal would come straight to us alleging that he was being threatened,' Navrátil said.

'I wonder…' Slonský said thoughtfully. 'Given the importance, Chvátal wouldn't wait to reply. He can't take the chance that Vitek will release the information to the press anyway. So if Vitek was killed on the fourteenth, the chances are that he contacted Chvátal a day or two before. Krob, have we got Vitek's mobile phone records?'

Krob riffled through the pages in front of him. 'Got them here, sir. I'll do a number look-up and see if I can find a link.'

Navrátil interrupted. 'Is there a number ending 3838?'

'Yes,' said Krob. 'Telephoned on the fourteenth at 09:28. And someone rang Vitek at 10:17.'

'It's the number Chvátal has on his website for enquiries. My guess is that someone took a message and Chvátal rang back later, perhaps when someone went for coffee. And he'd use his cell phone.'

Slonský was unusually energised. 'Right. Krob, see if you can verify that the number of the mobile phone belongs to Chvátal. If it does, ask Spehar to track it through that Saturday. Jerneková, get a recent picture of Chvátal and show it to Suková and Veselá. I know it's been twenty-three years, but see if they recognise him as the man they were with. Peiperová, find out where Chvátal lives in case we need to arrest him.'

'And what should I do?' asked Navrátil.

Slonský became aware of a faux pas. 'You? You can't do anything. You're running the case.'

Acutely aware that he had trespassed on Navrátil's prerogative, Slonský decided to set up an alternative command centre in the bar down the road. Since this often doubled as Valentin's office there was every chance that the two would meet up, as indeed they did.

'Can you keep a secret?' Slonský asked.

'You need to ask me that? Journalists are notoriously close-mouthed.'

'Yes, but I'm asking you.'

'If you offend me I'm giving this brandy back.'

'What do you make of Petr Chvátal?'

'You're not planning on voting for him, are you?' Valentin asked, visibly shocked.

'I don't vote for anyone,' said Slonský. 'I always vote against people.'

'How do you mean?'

'I go down the lists looking for the ones I can't vote for, and if there's anyone left after that I vote for them.'

'And has anyone you've ever voted for actually won an election?'

'Of course not. Not every voter is as discriminating as me.'

'Chvátal is an opportunist. He's changed parties so many times. He cultivates a man of the people, Mr Average Czech, your best mate kind of image. Now that the Christian Democrats and the Catholic parties are falling apart he's positioned himself as their successor, believing in the same things but not connected with the Church. His party is polling quite well in South Moravia, but that's probably because the folks there know a root vegetable when they see one, and he's a complete turnip. No chance in Prague. Why do you ask?'

'He's got a past. You can't write anything about this, but he was active in the StB.'

'Active? How?'

'You don't want to know.'

'I definitely do. Judging by your unwillingness to tell me, he was either a trained assassin or he cheated at cards.'

'Worse than that.'

'What's worse than being a trained assassin or cheating at cards?'

'How about seducing women to order?'

'Is that a job?' Valentin asked. 'Why weren't we told that by the careers folk at school?'

'You may not believe this, but the StB had a hotel room specially rigged up for filming illicit encounters.'

'Of course they did,' Valentin replied.

'You knew?'

'You didn't have to be too bright to spot that, Josef. Blackmail pictures often featured the same views out of the windows. Besides which, shifting photographic equipment around town would be cumbersome. Much better to set up a professional studio and kid people it's an ordinary hotel bedroom.'

Slonský felt rather put out that Valentin had known this and not mentioned it. The fact that he had not asked did not mitigate the feeling to any degree. 'Anyway, Chvátal used to take women there whom the StB wanted to blackmail.'

'Did he? Some blighters get all the luck.'

'It's morally despicable.'

'Yes — yes, of course it is. Goes without saying. I wasn't approving of the principle.'

They gulped their beers in silence for a while before a thought came to Valentin. 'You were asking about Halina Veselá the other day. Was she one of them?'

'Hush! I can't tell you that.'

'She was, wasn't she? As soon as you confirm it I'll get busy on a hatchet job for the paper on Chvátal. Thanks for the tip-off.'

'I haven't given you a tip-off.'

'Of course you haven't,' Valentin agreed with an exaggerated wink.

'I can understand why they'd try to entrap Veselá, but I can't quite fathom the first woman.'

'I can't help you there unless you tell me who it is.'

'I'm not going to do that. She deserves her privacy. But for all she was proud of her status twenty-three years ago, I can't see why the StB would be interested in her.'

'Maybe they weren't.'

'Come again?'

'Maybe they'd just set up the room and wanted to give the equipment a trial run.'

Slonský grabbed Valentin's head and planted a kiss on the top again.

'Will you stop doing that? People are looking.'

'I'm sure you're right! That's why the StB handed the film and photos over to Vitek. They never really wanted them in the first place. He told the woman a cock and bull story about having bought them and then punishing the blackmailers. More likely he guessed what must have happened, went to see his StB contacts, told them someone was trying to extort money from her using StB materials, probably said if they didn't act there was a risk everyone would find out about the cameras in that room, which would make the whole project useless, and they handed them over to keep him quiet.'

'I bet they kept copies somewhere though.'

'No doubt about that. But if Chvátal had anything to do with the extortion attempt there'll be a reprimand somewhere in the files. If there's one thing the StB didn't like, it was private enterprise.'

When Slonský returned to his office he was buoyed up by the team's progress after a horrible, bitty enquiry.

'You're looking chirpy,' said Mucha.

'It's spring. The birds are singing, the breweries are in full production, you're staying and all is right with the world.'

'I warn you, if you're going to go around spreading happiness recklessly, I may reconsider my decision to stay on.'

'I want you to do that voodoo that you do so well,' Slonský said.

'If you're going to sing Sinatra again I'll definitely reconsider. What do you want?'

'I'll bet that somewhere in the files there's a reprimand from the StB to Petr Chvátal, probably around May or June 1986. What do you reckon?'

'I'm ahead of you. I didn't see a reprimand, but he was questioned about the actions of his handler and made a statement.'

'And it says?'

'Hang on, I'll see if I can find it again. There you are. He took an unauthorised target to a meeting place and thereby jeopardised the security of its location. His defence was that his boss told him to find someone, so he took a woman he was involved with at the time. No name mentioned.'

'Thank you! Just what I suspected. There'll be a cup of coffee and the pastry of your choice waiting for you in the canteen.'

'Are you going to pay for it, or should I take my wallet?'

Krob and Navrátil were waiting with equally good news.

'Spehar can confirm that Chvátal, or at least his mobile phone, was within fifty metres of Vitek's flat on the afternoon of 14th February,' Krob began.

'That's a good start,' Slonský agreed.

'It gets better,' Navrátil asserted. 'We've got him on a traffic camera heading into the street where Vitek lived.'

Slonský nodded. 'So we can place him near to the crime scene at the time we think the crime was committed. That's good, but a confession but would be better. Let's bring him in and see if we can get one. But be discreet when you pick him up. I want him to think you're the nice guys.'

'What does that make you?' Navrátil laughed.

'The stuff of nightmares. I think I play that part rather well.'

CHAPTER 21

There were probably no politer police in Prague than Navrátil and Krob. Having apologised for any inconvenience they may be causing, Navrátil asked Chvátal to come with them. Chvátal appeared reluctant, but Navrátil went on to say that it was not really a request and that, if necessary, they were prepared to arrest and handcuff him, but if he were to tell his secretary that he was just going out for a while they would wait for him outside so as not to create a scene.

Being polite does not necessarily mean being naïve, so when Chvátal attempted to sneak out of the back door he found Krob waiting there.

'The building is confusing, isn't it, sir?' he said. 'I think the front door is that way.'

Chvátal and Krob sat in the back as Navrátil negotiated the Prague traffic.

'I don't know what you want with me,' Chvátal protested. 'I've haven't done anything.'

'As soon as we've established that you'll be on your way back then,' Krob said. 'Needless to say, we'll arrange transport in those circumstances.'

'Aren't you going to tell me what this is about so I can clear it up quickly?'

'We need to conduct a formal interview with safeguards for your interests, sir. You'll hear it all when we get to the station.'

Chvátal was shown to the interview room, told his rights and given a coffee, then, on Slonský's instructions, left to stew for fifteen minutes before Navrátil and Slonský entered the room.

'You're quite sure you don't want a lawyer present?' asked Navrátil.

'Why should he need a lawyer if he's innocent?' Slonský asked.

'I haven't done anything,' Chvátal insisted again.

'I'm pleased to hear that,' said Slonský. 'It gives us so much less work if we don't have to prepare cases against people for the prosecutor. Nevertheless, I'm sure you can understand we can't just take your word for that.'

'Then let's get on with it,' said Chvátal, folding his arms in a defiant pose.

'We're investigating —' began Navrátil.

'Just a moment,' Slonský interrupted. 'We need Officer Krob too. He'll only be a minute or two.'

'Of course,' said Navrátil, not quite sure why Krob had been told to wait outside until he was called. After a suitable interval Slonský went to the door and yelled down the corridor.

'Look lively, Krob. We mustn't keep Mr Chvátal waiting.'

Krob took his seat amidst profuse apologies while Slonský sat behind Chvátal, thus ensuring that Chvátal was being questioned from two sides and had to keep turning.

'We're investigating the suspicious death of Dominik Vitek,' Navrátil announced. 'We believe that you can assist us in those enquiries.'

'Dominik Vitek?'

'Do you know him?'

Chvátal hesitated. If he said yes he would be in for deeper questioning, and if he said no and they knew otherwise he would be in for even deeper questioning. 'I knew him some time ago.'

'Can you remember when you last saw him?'

'I meet so many people as a public figure. I can't be expected to know all of them.'

'I've got a photo of him if that helps,' Slonský said, leaning forward to hand it to Chvátal. 'Sorry, it's one from the morgue, but at least it's well-focused.'

Chvátal winced. Slonský could see that his hand was trembling.

'Sadly nobody found him for a while — not until the smell was bad enough to upset the neighbours, hence the funny colour of his face,' Slonský added.

'The thing is, Mr Chvátal,' Navrátil said calmly, 'we know that Vitek was killed on the afternoon of 14th February, and we also know that he telephoned you in the morning and that you telephoned him back at 10:17. Would you mind telling us what he wanted to talk to you about?'

'I'm standing for election at the next opportunity. Mr Vitek wanted to discuss an aspect of our programme. Unfortunately, he had misunderstood it, so it was important that I should ring him back at the first opportunity to put him right.'

'What aspect was that?'

Chvátal smirked. 'I'm sure I don't need to tell you that Mr Vitek was a homosexual. He was concerned that our clear focus on family values meant that we would propose punitive anti-gay measures.'

'It's odd that you should say that we wouldn't need to be told that Mr Vitek was a homosexual,' Slonský growled, 'given that we have absolutely no evidence of any relationships of any kind for him. Nor does he seem to have been active in any specifically gay rights campaign, though he had liberal views in many respects, at least until somebody beat his brains out. He was opposed to capital punishment, for example, which will probably benefit his murderer.'

Chvátal's smirk faded.

'And this misunderstanding was so important that you felt that you had to go to his flat that afternoon?' Navrátil asked.

Chvátal span back to face forwards. 'I'm sorry?' he said.

'Is that an apology for killing him?' Slonský blurted out.

'No! No, I just wondered why you thought I went round to see him.'

'To be fair,' said Slonský, 'we know that your mobile phone went to see him. I suppose you could have lent it to someone and got it back after the killing.'

Chvátal was gripping the edge of the table tightly.

'As for you,' Slonský continued, 'we have you on camera a little way down the street heading in the direction of the flat.' He handed Chvátal another photograph. 'You look a bit tense here. Bad journey on the Metro?'

'I think I'd like a lawyer now,' Chvátal whispered.

'I bet you would. However, you're just assisting us with our enquiries at the moment. You're not entitled to a lawyer until we arrest you.'

'Arrest me then, or let me go.'

'As you wish. Krob, when you take Mr Chvátal back don't forget to put the lights and siren on so everyone sees you coming and gets out of your way. But before we do that, Mr Chvátal, please show us your right knee.'

'My knee? What is this nonsense?'

'I liked a game of hockey myself when I was younger. I wasn't especially skilful but when I hammered someone into the boards they knew about it. I expect you know how that feels.' Slonský dived forward and pushed Chvátal's trouser leg up. 'An old hockey scar. That's not a surprise, because I have some more photographs here in which you can see a scar exactly like that. Actually, you can see a whole lot more than that. We got these from Mr Vitek's flat, and this is what he wanted to talk to you about.'

Chvátal took just one glance and turned away again.

'You were quite a lad back then, weren't you?' Slonský continued. 'There can't be too many young men who earn their living screwing women, especially not as a matter of state security. You see, we know you worked for the StB. We have your personnel record.'

Chvátal seemed deflated.

'I don't really need your confession,' Slonský went on. 'I can tell you what happened. Vitek rang you to tell you to withdraw from the election or he would release the photos and ruin your reputation for old-fashioned family values. You tried to talk him round, he wouldn't be swayed, so you hit him with a cast iron frying pan and then tried to find the photographs in his apartment. Except that they weren't there, of course. He'd put them in secure offsite storage.' Slonský shook his head. 'Why didn't you just withdraw gracefully instead of killing an inoffensive old man?'

'Inoffensive old man?' screeched Chvátal. 'That shows what you know.' He rose from his chair and turned to face Slonský, his face contorted in his fury. 'He was just as involved as I was. He was my handler!'

Slonský somehow managed not to look as surprised as he felt. 'Tell us about it,' he said.

'The whole thing was his idea. His cabaret was tolerated because the government wanted it to look as if it could laugh at itself, but when Halina Veselá started writing they couldn't take that any longer. Vitek didn't want a crackdown on dissent. It would have ruined him. The original plan was to eliminate her. She'd be found in her flat having been electrocuted by a faulty hairdryer or iron. She wouldn't have been the first. Vitek said they didn't need to do that, and it would only make her a martyr. He could get her to stop writing by discrediting her. He got a hotel room rigged up, then he told me to give it a trial run to check everything recorded clearly.

'I took a woman I was involved with at the time, a married woman who I thought might pay me a bit for the pictures, especially if someone else made the demand and I encouraged her not to cause us both to be exposed. When Vitek saw the pictures he went ape. He knew the woman. He demanded I hand them over and shut up about it all, but we'd invested too much time and money to call the plan off, so a few days later I took Veselá there. He got me the drugs I gave her. He was as involved as I was. But suddenly he's playing the high and mighty guardian of justice! Telling me that he'd make sure the photos ended my career if I didn't end it myself. I'd invested too much in remaking myself to let that happen.'

Slonský stood up and pushed his chest against Chvátal's. 'Sit down, and think of a lawyer you know. Navrátil will charge you now.'

Navrátil stapled the sheets together and slid them into an envelope. 'Sir,' he said, 'was everybody working for the StB back then?'

'Not quite everyone,' Slonský replied. 'I didn't, and Lukas didn't. There may have been one or two more. I'm pretty sure your mother didn't, for example.'

'So was Vitek a good guy or a bad guy?' Jerneková demanded to know.

'Just a guy like anyone else, I suppose. He kept the StB off his back by doing bits of work for them. I think The Ladies' Lounge was genuinely a good thing. Life was miserable for a lot of us men back then, so God knows what it was like for women. They needed that place.'

'I'd never have had you down as a feminist,' Peiperová admitted.

'I've always had a lot of time for women,' Slonský said. 'My mother was one, you know.'

'A feminist?'

'No, a woman.'

'Maybe we still need a place like that today,' Jerneková mused. 'A place where you can go for a night out and not get hands all over you.'

'Goodness, Lucie,' said Peiperová, 'what kind of places are you going to?'

'Wrestling and judo mostly. Occasional bit of Thai kickboxing. There's nothing quite like watching two guys kicking each other in the conkers for taking your mind off things.'

The clock in the foyer ticked to the top of the hour. Sergeant Mucha laid down his pen and donned his coat to go home.

'Fancy a beer?' came a voice from the shadows.

'My wife will be expecting me.'

'A beer doesn't have to take long. I'll put you in a taxi afterwards,' said Slonský.

'I know what'll happen. You and that pal of yours will ply me with free drink and before you know it I'll be rolling home after eleven and coming into work tomorrow with a stinking hangover.'

'I know,' said Slonský. 'Great, isn't it?'

A NOTE TO THE READER

Dear Reader,

I do not have comprehensive knowledge of Prague's clubs, so I will add my usual disclaimer that this is a work of fiction and any similarity of name is entirely coincidental. However, the story was spurred by a visit to an entirely different European city where I saw a sign to The Ladies' Lounge over a doorway. Neither is there any connection to the support group for women in Torquay who have suffered abuse. You can read about — and support — their work at www.ladies-lounge.co.uk.

Slonský is not yet ready to retire. He probably never will be, though it may be forced upon him one day. The more interest there is in his activities, the more likely another volume is, so please encourage your friends to read his adventures!

If you have enjoyed this novel, I'd be really grateful if you would leave a review on **Amazon** and **Goodreads**. I love to hear from readers, so please keep in touch through **Facebook, Threads** or **Twitter/X**, or leave a message on my **website**. I'd love you to subscribe to my newsletter there.

Všechno nejlepší!
Graham Brack

Sapere Books is an exciting new publisher of brilliant fiction and popular history.

To find out more about our latest releases and our monthly bargain books visit our website:
saperebooks.com

www.ingramcontent.com/pod-product-compliance
Lightning Source LLC
LaVergne TN
LVHW041248080426
835510LV00009B/647